ANGRY BIRDS™
TRANSFORMERS®

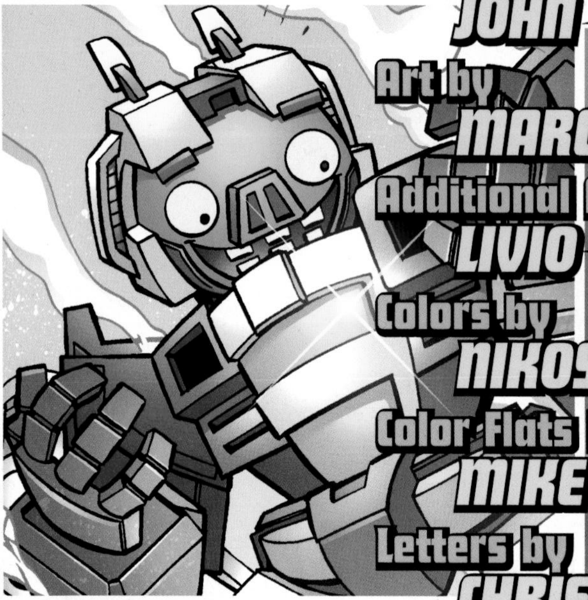

Written by
JOHN BARBER

Art by
MARCELO FERREIRA

Additional Art by
LIVIO RAMONDELLI

Colors by
NIKOS KOUTSIS

Color Flats by
MIKE TORIS

Letters by
CHRIS MOWRY AND SHAWN LEE

Series Edits by
DAVID HEDGECOCK

Laura Nevanlinna, Publishing Director
Jukka Heiskanen, Editor-in-Chief, Comics
Juha Mäkinen, Editor, Comics
Jan Schulte-Tigges, Art Director, Comics
Henri Sarimo, Graphic Designer

HC: 978-1-63140-258-6 TPB: 978-1-63140-421-4

18 17 16 15 1 2 3 4

IDW® Licensed By: Hasbro

www.IDWPUBLISHING.com
IDW founded by Ted Adams, Alex Garner, Kris Oprisko, and Robbie Robbins

Facebook: facebook.com/idwpublishing
Twitter: @idwpublishing
YouTube: youtube.com/idwpublishing
Instagram: instagram.com/idwpublishing
deviantART: idwpublishing.deviantart.com
Pinterest: pinterest.com/idwpublishing/idw-staff-faves

Originally published as ANGRY BIRDS TRANSFORMERS issues #1–4.

Cover by
MARCELO FERREIRA
Cover Colors by
NIKOS KOUTSIS
Collection Edits by
JUSTIN EISINGER AND
ALONZO SIMON
Collection Design by
THOM ZAHLER

SPECIAL THANKS TO
JUKKA HEISKANEN,
JUHA MAKINEN, AND THE
ROVIO TEAM FOR THEIR
HARD WORK AND
INVALUABLE
ASSISTANCE.

CHAPTER 1

Art by Marcelo Ferreira • Colors by Nikos Koutsis

OUR WAR HAS RAGED FOR EONS.
HEROIC AUTOBOT VERSUS EVIL DECEPTICON. AND AT THE CENTER OF THE CONFLICT—THE ALLSPARK.
THE SOURCE OF LIFE FOR OUR KIND. THE SOURCE OF LIFE FOR...
THE TRANSFORMERS
MORE THAN MEETS THE EYE!
I AM OPTIMUS PRIME, LEADER OF THE AUTOBOTS... PROTECTOR OF THE ALLSPARK.
AND TODAY... OUR RESOLVE WILL BE TESTED LIKE NEVER BEFORE.
BOOM
ENGINES ARE OUT, PRIME!
BOOM
LOOKS LIKE WE AIN'T GOIN' NO PLACE—BOSSMAN, WE'RE SITTIN' DEAD IN SPACE!
BOOM
BOOM
THE BATTLE IS FAR FROM OVER, JAZZ—INITIATE AN EMERGENCY QUANTUM JUMP.
I HEAR YA—BUT WE DON'T GOT ENOUGH TIME!
IF MEGATRON GETS HIS HANDS ON THE ALLSPARK, HE WILL CREATE AN UNSTOPPABLE ARMY... AND THE GALAXY WILL FALL.
WE HAVE TO MAKE ENOUGH TIME.
BUMBLEBEE—THE ALLSPARK MUST BE PROTECTED AT ALL COST. WITHOUT IT, WE ARE THE LAST OF OUR KIND.
THE FUTURE OF CYBERTRON IS IN YOUR HANDS, OLD FRIEND.
GOTCHA, OPTIMUS—NO PRESSURE!
I WISH WE NEVER HAD TO FIGHT—BUT YOU KNOW YOU CAN COUNT ON ME!
PREPARE TO HOLD THEM OFF, AUTOBOTS—
VROOOM

—OUR HULL HAS BEEN BREACHED!
ATTACK, MY DECEPTICONS!
DESTROY THE AUTOBOTS—AND TAKE THE ALLSPARK! WITH IT I SHALL RULE THE UNIVERSE!
AS YOU COMMAND, MEGATRON. OPERATION: DESTRUCTION!
"YES, MEGATRON. WHATEVER YOU SAY, MEGATRON."
SOUNDWAVE—YOU'RE SUCH A COMPANY MAN. YOU HAVE TO LEARN TO LOOSEN UP!
PROCEED LOGICALLY, STARSCREAM. ATTACK PLAN OMEGA DELTA.
SORRY, SHOCKWAVE—
WHK-
WHEK-
WHEK-
WHK-
WHK
—BUT STARSCREAM'S GOT OTHER IDEAS!
ZAPP
ZAPP
ZAPP

MIGHT GO EASY ON YOU!
WELL, TO BE HONEST, I PROBABLY WON'T.
SO, I GUESS... RUN TO YOUR SPARK'S CONTENT. IT WON'T HELP.
EEP!
STARSCREAM—DO NOT DESERT YOUR PO—BLURGGG!
SPLOOSH
SORRY, 'CONS. MAYBE TODAY ISN'T YOUR DAY, AFTER ALL!
AUTOBOTS—HEATWAVE HAS FOUND A HOLE IN THEIR DEFENSES! PRESS THE ADVANTAGE!
STARSCREAM, YOU FOOL! I HAD A PLAN!
THOOM
ALMOST GOT IT! KEEP ON KEEPIN' ON!
YOU HAD A PLAN, MEGATRON? WELL, I HAVE AMBITION!
GET BACK TO YOUR POST! IF YOU CAUSE US TO FAIL, STARSCREAM—
YEAH, YEAH—WHOOPS!
GUYS—STOP HIM!
YOU BRING DISHONOR WITH YOUR UNENDING TREACHERY, DECEPTICON.
SLIIICE
FA-WHOOOSH
BIG WORDS, DRIFT—ME GRIMLOCK SAY "JUST ROAST THE SUCKER!"
I'D LOVE TO STAY AND CHAT—
—CONVERSATIONS WITH YOU ARE ALWAYS SO ENLIGHTENING—
—BUT I'VE GOT A LITTLE YELLOW TWERP TO CATCH!

CHOOM
I GOT IT, PRIME! QUANTUM ENGINE IS SPOOLED—
—WE'RE READY TO JUMP!
PRIME, YOU COWARD—
KRONK
ON MY SIGNAL, JAZZ!
HEATWAVE—GET THESE DECEPTI-CREEPS OFF MY SHIP!
BLURRBB
I GOT 'EM, OPTIMUS!
A COUPLE MILLION POUNDS OF WATER PRESSURE OUGHT TO CLEAR THE DECK!
SPLOOSH
WAM WAM
ME GRIMLOCK SAY "OPEN DOOR!"
SURE. ONE MINUTE.
NOW, BUMBLEBEE—WHERE WERE WE...?
HANG ON, STARSCREAM! WE CAN DEAL WITH THIS LIKE RATIONAL CREATURES!
"RATIONAL CREATURES"... NO, THAT WASN'T IT...
...OH, YES—I WAS GOING TO BLAST YOU, TAKE THE ALLSPARK, AND CONQUER THE UNIVERSE FOR MYSELF.
JAZZ—ENGAGE QUANTUM JUMP!

BLAAFF
KSSSSHH
YIKES!
NO! THE ALLSPARK— TUMBLING INTO A QUANTUM TUNNEL!
IT'LL BE LOST FOREVER!
I HAD IT IN MY GRASP!
WHAT ABOUT THIS IS HARD TO GRASP, CHUCK?
THEY TOOK OUR EGGS, WE HAVE TO GET 'EM BACK. AND LIKE ALWAYS—THEY'LL BE LOOKING FOR US.
WE WON'T STOP LOOKING 'TIL WE FIND THE ALLSPARK, STARSCREAM. AS FOR YOU—EVER HEAR THE OLD EARTH SAYING—
"—A BIRD IN THE HAND IS WORTH TWO IN THE BUSH"?
I'M SAYING, RED—
—WE'RE NOT WORTH ANYTHING HIDING BEHIND THIS BUSH!
IT'S A CACTUS, CHUCK—
—AND WHAT WAS THAT NOISE?
WHO CARES, RED?
NONE OF US IS HAPPY ABOUT THE PIGS GETTIN' OUR EGGS. FACT IS, YOU COULD SAY WE'RE ALL—
WHUMP

ANGRY BIRDS™
CHUCK, HOLD ON—I HAVE A PLAN!
DON'T THINK CHUCK'S LISTENING. YOU KNOW HOW HE GETS.
I HATE IT WHEN THE BIG GUYS ARGUE!
YOU SAID IT!
WE SHOULD BE FIGHTING THE PIGS, NOT EACH OTHER!
WHO'S FIGHTING? STELLA, YA MIND EXPLAININ'?
BUBBLES, JUST CONCENTRATE ON THE MISSION—
—BECAUSE READY OR NOT, HERE WE COME!
YA-HOOOOO!
KA-SMASH
TNT
TNT
TNT

CARUUUUSH
HIYA—HOPE I'M NOT INTERRUPTING DINNER!
BIRDS!
WHY CAN'T YOU LET ME EAT IN PEACE?!
GRAB THE EGGS! WE HAVE TO GET OUT OF HERE!
COME ON, GUYS, WE'VE GOT TO RESCUE THOSE EGGS BEFORE THIS WHOLE PLAN—
—FALLS APART!
LEAVE THOSE EGGS ALONE—
—UH-OH.
KA-CHUCK
BWA-KOOOM

STUPID, STUPID LITTLE BIRDS!
ALL THEY DID IS DELAY MY MEAL! AND I WASN'T EVEN HUNGRY!
YOU SAID YOU WERE STARVING, KING PIG!
SILENCE, MINION!
I HAD SPECIFIC SPECIFICATIONS FOR CONSTRUCTION!
IF YOU MINIONS FOLLOWED ORDERS, IT WOULD'VE STOOD UP AGAINST ANY BIRD!
UH, LIKE ALL YOUR OTHER KNOCKED-DOWN BUILDINGS?
WHY, YOU—
NEXT TIME, FOREMAN PIG!
NOW, MINIONS—CARRY, CARRY, CARRY!
CHEF—THINK OF A TASTY OMELET RECIPE... BECAUSE I'M READY TO BREAK A FEW EGGS!
UNNNFF...
RED—THEY'RE GETTING AWAY WITH THE EGGS!
I KNOW—BUT WE'VE GOT TO MAKE SURE EVERYBODY'S OKAY!
TERENCE, BOMB—YOU UNDER THERE?
BOOM
RIGHT HERE, BOSS. I'M FINE. TERENCE IS...
...WELL, TERENCE.
...
AND CHUCK...
SORRY, GUYS—I THOUGHT I HAD IT.
I'LL LET YOU HAVE IT, CHUCK!
THIS ISN'T A GAME—WE'VE GOT TO RESCUE THE EGGS, AND THE PIGS HAVE A HEAD START! THE FIVE OF US—
FIVE? IF THERE'S ONLY FIVE OF US—

"—THEN WHERE ARE THE BLUES?"
MOVE IT, GUYS!
THEY'RE GONNA BE MAD WHEN THEY FIND OUT WE RAN OFF!
WE DIDN'T RUN OFF—WE'RE SAVING THE DAY!
IS THAT HAL?
YEAH!
AND HE'S ALL ALONE.
AN' THAT'S JUST HOW I PLAN ON STAYIN', LITTLE FELLAS.
I GOT MY BANJO HERE TO KEEP ME COMPANY.
BUT HAL!
THE PIGS!
YEAH!
LITTLE BUDDIES, I DON'T WANNA GET INVOLVED IN BIRD VERSUS PIGS. THAT'S NOT MY SCENE, DUDES.
BUT THE PIGS TOOK THE EGGS!
THEY'RE GONNA EAT 'EM!
NO THEY'RE NOT—WE'RE GONNA STOP 'EM!
!!
YOU KIDS ARE GONNA STOP THE PIGS ALONE?
WE'RE NOT KIDS!
WELL, YOU'RE ALSO NOT GOIN' ALONE.
COME ON, COMPADRES—LET'S SEE A PIG ABOUT SOME EGGS.
YAY!
THANKS, HAL!
YOU'RE A BIRD AMONG BIRDS!
EASY, GUYS. I JUST WANNA GET THIS OVER WITH—

"—SO THINGS CAN GET BACK TO NORMAL!"
...OR WE COULD MIX IN SOME EXTRA EGGS TO THE OMELET.
AND MAYBE ADD TO IT A SIDE OF EGGS...
...MMMM. EGGS.
YOU SHOULDN'T PUT ALL YOUR EGGS IN ONE OMELET.
WHAT WAS THAT, CHEF PIG?
I SAID, WHERE IS THAT SMOKE COMING FROM?
THAT DOESN'T EVEN SOUND LIKE WHAT YOU SAID.
WHAT SMOKE—
—YIKES—
—THAT SMOKE! I MEAN—
—THAT SMOKE IS WHAT I'VE BEEN LEADING US TO.
RIGHT?
YES!
YES, KING!
YES INDEEDY!
OF COURSE, SIR!
HMPH!
YEP!
ABSOLUTELY, KING, BUT... AH... ER...
..WHY, IF I MIGHT ASK?
AH. WELL.
YES.
NO—YOU SHOULDN'T ASK—
—BUT SINCE YOU DID... WHERE SMOKE IS...
...UM...
WHERE THERE'S SMOKE, THERE'S FIRE!
WHAT A GREAT IDEA—YOU NEED A FIRE TO COOK AN OMELET!
YES!
WHY—YES!
YES, YOU DO.

HM.
IT'S NOT FIRE.
BUT... IT MIGHT BE HOT.
SNORT.
SNORT-SNORT.
SNORK-BWAHHHHHHH!
ALL THE KNOCKED-OVER TREES AND ROCKS AND CACTUSES—
UH. WHAT ARE YOU DOING?
CACTI.
—THEM, TOO! I GET SO SAD WHEN I SEE PIGGY ISLAND HURT!
BWAHHHHHHH!
YEAH. THAT'S TRUE.
IT'S SAD.
I LOVE THIS PLACE.
WELL, SURE, YES—BUT LET'S GET BACK ON-TASK!
MY OMELET!
I DON'T KNOW IF THIS... THIS...
...
...SURE, OMELET COOKER, IS ACTUALLY HOT.
OMELET COOKER.
FIND OUT!
—HERE GOES NOTHING.
SNOUT
GOOD IDEA! SEE IF IT'S HOT, MINION!
BUT-BUT-BUT—!
BONK

FWASH
WOW!
I HAVE ARMS AND LEGS!
YUCK! DISGUSTING... THE WAY YOU WALK AND... AND... HAVE ARMS.
THERE OUGHTTA BE A LAW!
HEY! I—I AM WALKING!
PLUS I FEEL LIKE—I KNOW STUFF! THAT THING'S CALLED THE EGGSPARK—
—AND NOW I CAN DO ALL KINDS OF THINGS!
PEW
SPAK
WHAT HAPPENED TO NOT WANTING TO SEE PIGGY ISLAND GET HURT?!
THERE'S MORE... I CAN FEEL SOMETHING ELSE...
...LIKE I CAN CHANGE...
WHK-WHEK-WHEK-WHK-WHK

SPONGG
UM... TRY THE HANDLE?
SURE, SURE...
DING-DING-DONG-DING
THAT'S NOT RIGHT!
AHH!
SPROUNK
YIIIEE!
LET ME TRY—
—LITTLE OF THAT—
—SOME OF...
WHK-WHEK-WHEK-WHK-WHK
...THIS!
COME BACK HERE, MINION!
I'M NO MINION ANYMORE! I AM—
STARSCREAM PIG!
AND I'LL BE BACK...
FOOOSH

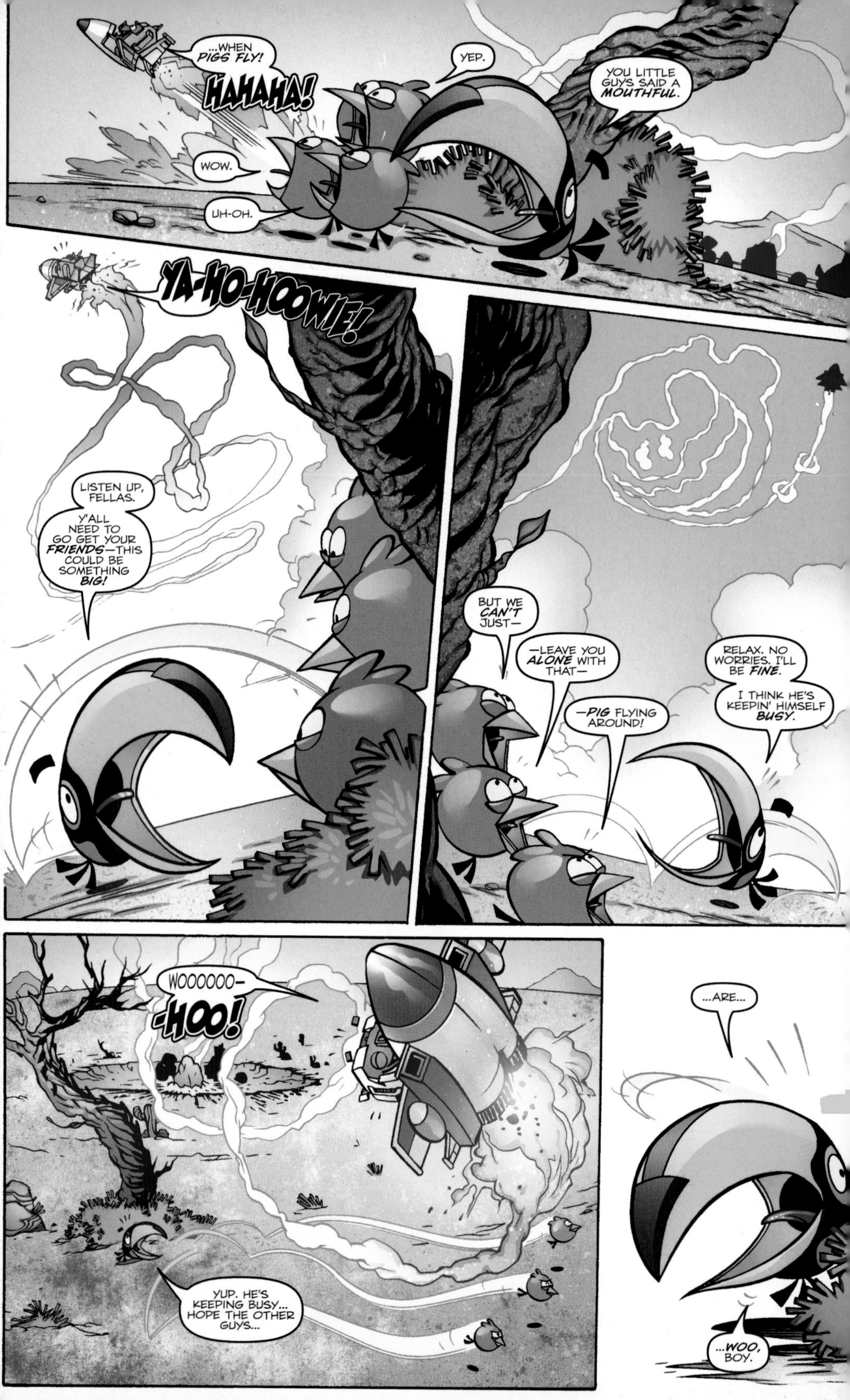

...WHEN *PIGS FLY!*

HAHAHA!

YEP.

YOU LITTLE GUYS SAID A ***MOUTHFUL***.

WOW.

UH-OH.

YA-HO-HOOWIE!

LISTEN UP, FELLAS.

Y'ALL NEED TO GO GET YOUR ***FRIENDS***—THIS COULD BE SOMETHING ***BIG!***

BUT WE ***CAN'T*** JUST—

—LEAVE YOU ***ALONE*** WITH THAT—

—***PIG*** FLYING AROUND!

RELAX. NO WORRIES. I'LL BE ***FINE***.

I THINK HE'S KEEPIN' HIMSELF ***BUSY***.

I FEEL... STRONG... SMART...
...BIG!
YES, YES—THAT'S RIGHT! I HEAR YOU!
GALVATRON PIG IS STRONGEST PIG THERE IS!
GRRR. THIS ISN'T RIGHT!
I ORDERED ALL MY PIECES TO GO INTO THE RIGHT PLACES LIKE I ALWAYS DO...
OPERATION: IMPOSITION.
KING—DO YOU STILL FUNCTION?
I AM NO LONGER A MERE KING—
—CALL ME MEGATRON PIG.
AND THESE ARMS AND LEGS...
...ARE ABSOLUTELY AS GROSS AS I THOUGHT THEY WOULD BE.
WALKING UPRIGHT. EW.

BLUUUUEES... WHERE ARE YOU?
EGGS— COME ON OUT, EGGS!
...
I'M WITH YOU, TERENCE. WE'RE WASTING TIME.
THERE— I SEE THE BLUES...
...AND IT LOOKS LIKE THEY HAVE SOMETHING IMPORTANT TO SAY!
WE FOUND THE EGGS AND—
—WOULD YOU BELIEVE—
—A PIG CAN FLY?!
ONLY IF IT HAS SOMETHING TO DO WITH THESE WEIRD GRAVITATIONAL FLUCTUATIONS...
ONE AT A TIME, GUYS—TELL US WHAT'S HAPPENED!
AN EGGSPARK!
A STARSCREAM PIG!
THE EGGS ARE IN DANGER!
DANGER?
THAT'S ALL I NEED TO HEAR. WHERE ARE THEY?
AT THE BASE OF THE SMOKE!

OKAY, GUYS—
—THIS ONE I DEFINITELY GOT!
CHUCK, WAIT! DON'T GO RACING OFF AGAIN, BUDDY.
THIS IS IT, CHUCK.
THIS IS YOUR CHANCE. YOU MESSED UP—
—NOW FIX IT!
HAL! WHAT ARE YOU DOING HERE?!
SLOW DOWN, AMIGO! TAKE A SECOND TO TAKE IT ALL IN!
NO WAY—
—THESE PIGS MADE A FOOL OF ME, AND I'M GONNA—
—WHOA!
BONK
I'M OUTTA CONTROL!
YOU AND ME BOTH, CHUCK!
FWASH

ME GRIMLOCK BIRD READY TO BUST SOME PIGS!
NOW, HANG ON. WE'RE ALL RATIONAL CREATURES.
LET'S TALK THIS OUT.
ME GRIMLOCK BIRD NO TALK...
...ME GRIMLOCK BIRD WONDERS WHAT HAPPENED...?
THE NAME'S BUMBLEBEE BIRD—
—AND I THINK IF WE ALL TRY TO BE NICE, WE WON'T HAVE TO FIGHT!
NOT FIGHT?
WE'RE DECEPTIHOGS! AND I MIGHT NOT KNOW MUCH ABOUT THESE NEW FORMS...
...BUT I'M PRETTY SURE I WOULDN'T CHANGE INTO THIS IF I DIDN'T WANT TO FIGHT.
WHK-WHEK-WHEK-WHK-WHK
ME GRIMLOCK BIRD SAY—
—"GET DOWN, BIRD!"
THOOM

YOU TRY HURT FRIEND BUMBLEBEE BIRD!
HA HA HA!
WHAT ARE YOU GONNA DO—
—POKE US WITH YOUR TINY LITTLE DINOSAUR ARMS?
FA-WHOOSH
ME GRIMLOCK BIRD'S—
OUCH.
—ARMS NOT—
FA-WHOOSH
FA-WHOOSH
—TINY LITTLE!
ME GRIMLOCK BIRD SAY YOU ARMS TINY LITTLE!
WHACK
OPERATION: EVASION!
QUIT MESSING AROUND, SOUNDWAVE PIG—
FWASH

—GRAB THE EGGS AND RUN, BEFORE THAT MANIAC BIRD MAKES US INTO OMELETS!
ME GRIMLOCK BIRD SAY "YOU BETTER RUN!"
OPERATION: EVACUATION!
THIS ISN'T RIGHT! SOMEBODY FIX ME!
ME GRIMLOCK BIRD SAY "JOB WELL DONE."
UH, GRIMLOCK BIRD, YOU DON'T NEED TO SAY YOUR NAME WHEN YOU...
...FORGET IT. THE BIG PROBLEM IS:
I THINK WE FORGOT SOMETHING IMPORTANT—
"—THE EGGS ARE GONE!"
KRAK
NEXT:
"AGE OF EGGSTINCTION" OR "OVER HARD!"

Art by Livio Ramondelli

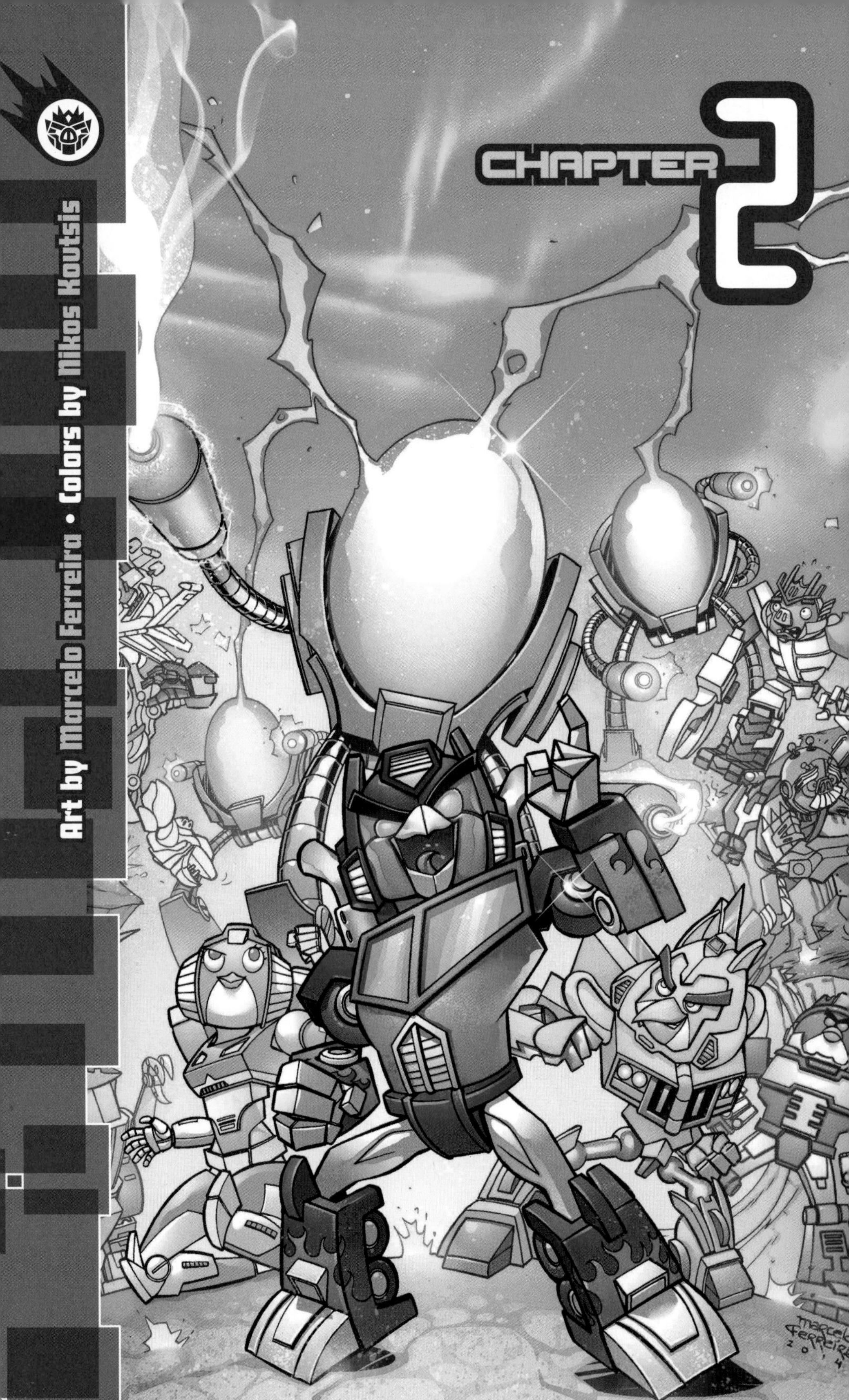
CHAPTER 2
Art by Marcelo Ferreira • Colors by Nikos Koutsis
MARCELO FERREIRA 2014

WHAT ON PIGGY ISLAND HAPPENED HERE?!
CHUCK, HAL—IS THAT YOU?
"ARE THAT YOU," YOU MEAN.
OR, ER, "ARE THEY YOU"?
HUH. YOU KNOW—
ARE YOU YOU?
ME GRIMLOCK BIRD SAY "ME GRIMLOCK BIRD NOT HAL"!
HE MEANS WELL.
HI, HI THERE, TINY FLYING FRIENDS! GOOD TO MEET YOU!
AGE OF EGGSTINCTION!

STELLA— WHAT ARE THOSE... THINGS UNDER CHUCK?
I'VE NEVER SEEN ANYTHING LIKE THEM.
THE NAME'S BUMBLEBEE BIRD—AND YOU KNOW I CAN HEAR YOU, RIGHT?
I KNOW— THEY'RE CALLED... WHAT WAS IT? BARNS AND PEGS?
...
YEAH, TERENCE IS RIGHT—IT'S "ARMS AND LEGS"!
WHATEVER IT IS, BOMB—IT'S WEIRD AND I DON'T LIKE IT!
ME GRIMLOCK BIRD SAY "IT DON'T MATTER WHAT YOU LIKE!"
ME GRIMLOCK BIRD SAY "WE GOTTA FIND THE EGGS."
GUY'S GOT A POINT. LET'S GET TOGETHER AND FIGURE OUT A PLAN.
CHUCK! HAVE YOU GONE CRAZY?!
YOU'VE NEVER PLANNED FOR ANYTHING IN YOUR LIFE!
YOU LITERALLY DO NOT KNOW HOW TO SPELL "PLAN"! I'VE SEEN YOU TRY!
I KINDA REMEMBER BEFORE I TOUCHED THE EGGSPARK. IT'S JUST TAKIN' A FEW MINUTES TO GET EVERYTHING SORTED OUT, MENTAL-WISE.
LIKE, I THINK I KNOW YOU, RED. WHAT'S YOUR NAME?
PAT PAT PAT
WHAT? YOU JUST SAID IT. MY NAME'S RED.
YOU DON'T HAVE TO PATRONIZE ME, LITTLE GUY.
NOBODY'S NAMED AFTER THEIR FEATHERS.

LISTEN TO GRIMLOCK BIRD!
EGGS ARE IN DANGER— AND PIGS ARE LIKE BUMBLEBEE BIRD AN' ME.
YOU'RE USELESS, BIRDS.
USELESS?!
HAL— YOU'RE OUR FRIEND!
YOU SAID YOU WANTED TO HELP US!
NOW ME GRIMLOCK BIRD SAYS YOU USELESS UNLESS YOU CAN DO THIS!
WHK-
WHEK
WHEK-
WHK-WHK
ME GRIMLOCK BIRD STILL GETTING HANG OF IT!
I DON'T SEE HOW THAT'S GONNA HELP.
MAYBE IF YOU WERE A MOTORCYCLE OR SOMETHING.
SERIOUSLY.
YIPE!
YIPE!
WHEK-
WHK
WHK
YIPE!

THIS BETTER!
THIS FORM LET ME GRIMLOCK BIRD RESCUE EGGS AND BE HERO!
AND YOU BIRDS—
—STAY OUTTA GRIMLOCK BIRD'S WAY!
HUH. THAT'S ACTUALLY A PRETTY GOOD MODE.
BETTER THAN A MOTORCYCLE.
NUH-UH. A MOTORCYCLE WOULD'VE BEEN COOLER.
OKAY, OKAY—
—CHUCK, I KNOW YOU'RE IN THERE SOMEWHERE, AND YOU'RE MY BEST FRIEND...
...CAN YOU DO THAT, TOO?
'COURSE I CAN. AND SO CAN YOU...
...IF YOU TOUCH THE EGGSPARK!
NOW, I'M NOT SUGGESTIN' YOU DO THIS WITHOUT CONSIDERIN' THE RAMIFICATIONS—
I CAN'T BELIEVE I'M HEARING THIS.
—BUT I THINK OUR FRIEND GRIMLOCK BIRD MIGHT HAVE A POINT—IF A SORTA POORLY VOCALIZED ONE.
THE PIGS ARE MORE POWERFUL THAN WE'VE EVER SEEN. AND THE EGGS DO NEED US.

AND THEY NEED US—
WHK- WHEK WHEK- WHK- WHK
—TO BE ABLE TO DO THIS.
I HATE TO SAY IT, BUT CHUCK SOUNDS REASONABLE.
I HATE THAT CHUCK SOUNDS REASONABLE. IT'S NOT NORMAL.
I THINK WE LEFT NORMAL BACK HOME WITH MATILDA.
WELL—I CAN'T ASK YOU TO DO THIS, BUT CHUCK—
BUMBLEBEE BIRD!
SORRY TO INTERRUPT.
—MIGHT BE RIGHT. WHO'S IN?
I'M WITH YOU.
OF COURSE!
...
WHAT HE SAID.
YOU CAN—
—COUNT ON—
—THE BLUES!
HERE GOES—
—EVERYTHING!
FWAASH

WELL, THIS IS NEAT-O.
BUT ME, JAZZ BIRD, I'D LIKE TO JUST CRUISE AROUND PIGGY ISLAND AND TAKE IN THE SIGHTS AND IF I'VE GOT TO FIGHT, WELL, I CAN LAY DOWN SOME SMOOTH GROOVES AN' MAKE THINGS HOT FOR THE NASTY PIGGIES!
WHY ARE YOU TALKING LIKE THAT?
HONOR AND CLARITY OF PURPOSE ARE THE ONLY COURSES OF ACTION FOR ME, DRIFT BIRD.
WITHIN EACH OF US LIES THE POTENTIAL FOR GREATNESS— THE METAPHOR OF THE EGG MANIFESTED IN THE PHYSICAL PLANE. ALSO, I CAN BLOW UP.
WHY DID YOU JUST SAY YOUR NAME FOR NO REASON?
... ...
HEY, REALLY, SERIOUSLY HEATWAVE BIRD, WHAT'S WITH ALL THE EXPOSITION?
FRANKLY, I, ARCEE BIRD, WOULD RATHER BE ANYWHERE THAN HANGING OUT WITH YOU JOKERS.
BUT SINCE WE'RE HERE— AND SINCE THE EGGS NEED US— I'LL RELY ON MY ENDLESS PATIENCE AND I'LL DICTATE THE MOST ADVANTAGEOUS COURSE OF ACTION.
THIS GAG IS REALLY WEARING THIN, GUYS.
ALRIGHT, ALRIGHT, WE'RE CALLED BLUESTREAK BIRD!
CAN WE STOP NOW?
THIS IS WHAT I WAS AFRAID OF. THEY'VE LOST THEIR MINDS.
DID THEY REALLY START WITH MUCH? PLUS, LOOK WHAT THEY GAINED!
BARNS AND PEGS?
SOMETHING LIKE THAT. ANYWAY— YOUR TURN, REDBIRD!
JUST RED. IT'S JUST...

...RED.
OOOH.
FWAAASSH
I... AM
OPTIMUS PRIME BIRD.
FATE RARELY CALLS UPON US AT A MOMENT OF OUR OWN CHOOSING—BUT FATE HAS CALLED UPON US NOW, OLD FRIENDS.
THE EGGS MUST BE RESCUED, THE PIGS MUST BE STOPPED, AND FREEDOM—THE RIGHT OF ALL SENTIENT BEINGS—MUST BE PROTECTED.
WE ACCEPT THIS BURDEN WITH ALL THAT WE ARE. FRIENDS—IT IS AN HONOR SERVING WITH YOU. NOW...
...AUTOBIRDS, TRANSFORM AND ROLL OUT!
UH, NICE SPEECH AN' ALL—
—BUT HOW DO YOU KNOW—
—WHERE WE'RE GOING?
SOMETIMES, BLUESTREAK BIRD, WE MUST HAVE FAITH...

"...AND ANSWERS WILL COME TO US."
I TELL YOU, THIS ISN'T RIGHT...
HUSH. I CAN'T HEAR THE VOICES IN MY HEAD.
THEY'RE GONNA FIND US, MEGATRON PIG—
—WE'VE GOTTA BE READY FOR THAT CRAZY DINO-BIRD'S ATTACK!
NO ONE HAS EVER DARED TO QUESTION MY AUTHORITY, STARSCREAM PIG!
WELL, I'M NOT LIKE EVERY OTHER PIG! IN FACT—
—MAYBE I SHOULD BE ORDERING YOU AROUND! I MEAN, WHO PUT YOU IN CHARGE OF THE DECEPTIHOGS IN THE FIRST PLACE?!
IT'S— IT'S LIKE HE'S SAYING EVERYTHING I FEEL!
HE'S GONNA GET IT. THIS ISN'T GONNA GO WELL FOR HIM.
NO, HE'S RIGHT—MAYBE LEADERSHIP SHOULD BE BASED ON MERIT, NOT—
WILL YOU THREE STIFLE IT BEFORE I HAVE YOU SMOOSHED FOR INSUBORDINATION?!
WELL, I DON'T LIKE THE SOUN OF THAT ONE BIT.
UH-OH.
WELP, I'M OUTTA HERE.
GOOD LUCK, FELLAS!
RMMMMMBBLLE

OHH, BOY. THIS AIN'T RIGHT, EITHER.
OPERATION: ELEVATION.
UH, YOU GUYS OKAY?
SILENCE, CRETINS. I NEED TO FIGURE OUT WHAT TO DO.
GALVATRON PIG KNOWS WHAT TO DO.
WHAT'S THAT?
YES, MY CONCLUSION EXACTLY—
—GALVATRON PIG SMASH!
NO, WAIT—!
BWUMPF
HUH—MAYBE I SHOULDN'T LISTEN TO THOSE VOICES IN MY HEAD.
CRACK

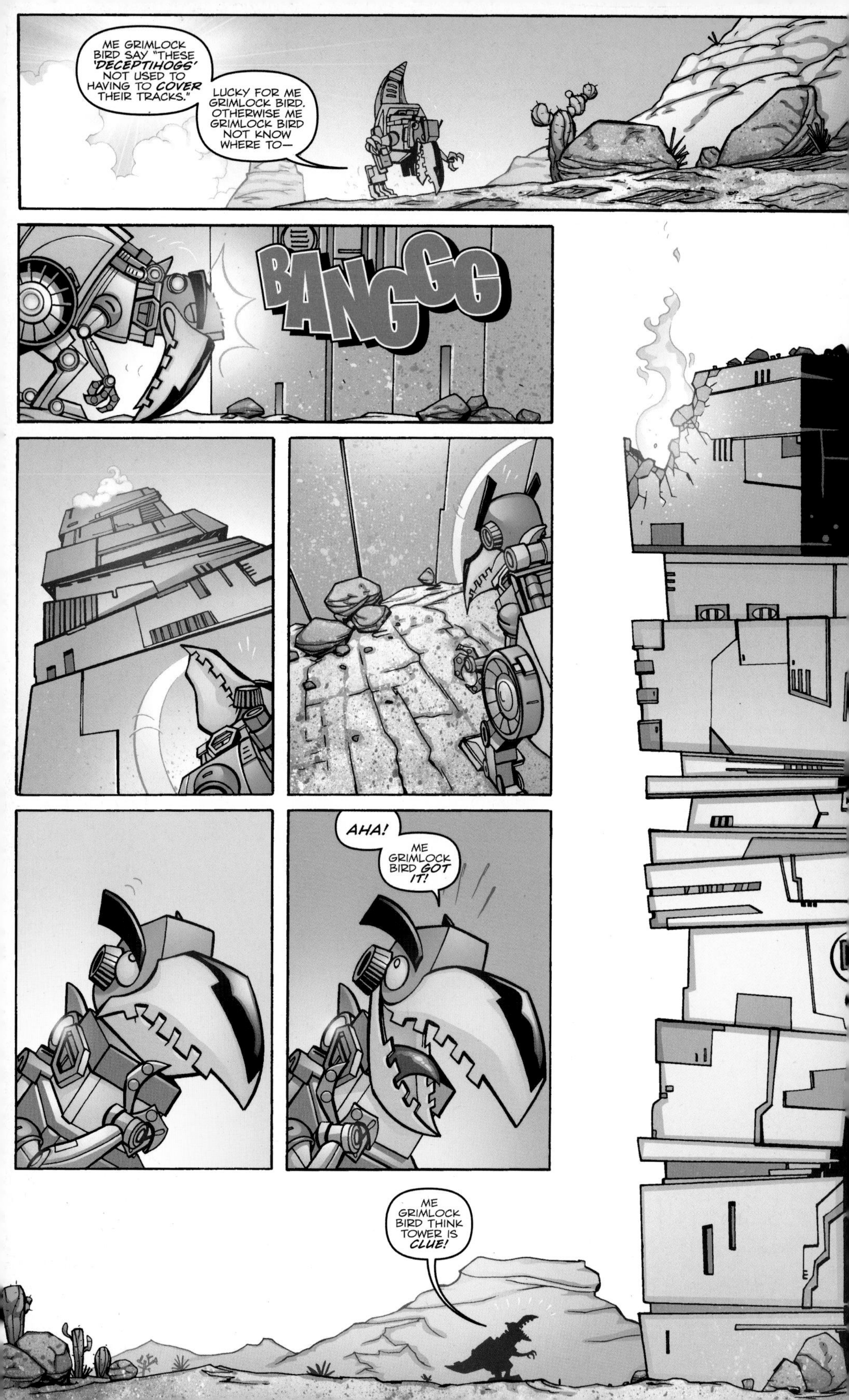

ME GRIMLOCK BIRD SAY "THESE 'DECEPTIHOGS' NOT USED TO HAVING TO COVER THEIR TRACKS."
LUCKY FOR ME GRIMLOCK BIRD. OTHERWISE ME GRIMLOCK BIRD NOT KNOW WHERE TO—
BANGGG
AHA!
ME GRIMLOCK BIRD GOT IT!
ME GRIMLOCK BIRD THINK TOWER IS CLUE!

UNNNG. HUF.
WHERE ARE WE?
SOMEBODY TURN ON A LIGHT.
THAT'S AN ORDER!
GYAH!
YUCK. I THOUGHT HAVING ARMS COULDN'T GET MORE GROSS...
...NOW, WHAT HAPPENED?
OPERATION: ILLUMINATION.
SOMEBODY HELP ME!
I BELIEVE WE FELL DOWN FROM THE TOP OF THE TOWER AND WE'RE STUCK HERE.
I CAN SEE THAT!
WELL, YOU ASKED.
THE QUESTION IS WHERE THIS THING CAME FROM?!
AND "HOW DO WE GET OUT?"
I BELIEVE, SIR, THAT IT WAS THE EGGSPARK. WE EACH GAINED THESE NEW FORMS WHEN WE TOUCHED THE EGGSPARK...
...AND THE EGGSPARK ITSELF IS TOUCHING PIGGY ISLAND.
HMM... IF EVERYTHING THAT TOUCHED THE EGGSPARK IS CHANGED, THAT MEANS...
NO! NOT PIGGY ISLAND!
NOT OUR HOME!
WHAT'LL WE DO?

ME GRIMLOCK BIRD SAY YOU GET SMOOSHED!
STOMP
THAT'S WHAT EVERYBODY SAYS!
TRY SOMETHING ORIGINAL!
YEAH!
YOU PIGS THOUGHT YOU HIDE FROM GRIMLOCK BIRD!
HOW DO YOU FIND THE TIME TO DO ANYTHING WHEN YOU KEEP SAYING YOUR NAME OVER AND OVER?
PAT
GRK
WHK-
WHEK
WHEK- WHK-
WHK
ENOUGH BLATHERING!
ALL I WANT TO DO IS EAT SOME EGGS! IS THAT SO MUCH TO ASK?
I'M HUNGRY— AND IT'S TIME TO GET COOKING!
THOM

WHY WON'T YOU STAND STILL?!
WOOOF
ME GRIMLOCK BIRD NOT KNOW HOW TO STAND STILL!
DON'T KNOW LOTS OF OTHER STUFF, TOO.
OPERATION: HUMILIATION.
THE AUTOBIRD IS MAKING FOOLS OF US, MASTER. BUT I HAVE A SECRET...
KAFF.
ENOUGH SECRETS! ENOUGH INCOMPETENCE!
SOMEBODY STOP THAT DINOSAUR!
NOBODY'S GONNA HELP ME...
...NOBODY'S QUALIFIED TO HELP ME...
...IT'S ALL DOWN TO LOCKDOWN PIG...?
FINE.
WHK WHEK WHEK WHK WHEK WHEK

THAT'S BETTER.
KONK
UM, ME GRIMLOCK BIRD DISAGREE WITH ASSESSMENT...
WELL, THAT WASN'T SO HARD.
I DON'T KNOW WHY YOU LOT WERE HAVING SO MUCH TROUBLE.
LET'S GET TO BUSINESS.
OPERATION: IMPOSITION.
MASTER— DO YOU TRUST LOCKDOWN PIG'S LOYALTIES?
I DON'T TRUST ANYBODY'S ANYTHING. WHAT DID YOU HAVE IN MIND?
MY SECRET. YOU SEE, THE EGGS...

THE EGGS ARE COMING WITH US, DECEPTIHOGS.
I DO NOT WANT TO FIGHT YOU, BUT IF YOU LEAVE ME NO CHOICE... I WILL.
YEAH, WE SHOULD TALK THIS OUT. WHAT'S OUR ARGUMENT, ANYWAY?
...
THEY STOLE THE EGGS, BUMBLEBEE BIRD.
WELL, THERE'S NO NEED TO RUSH INTO THINGS, HEATWAVE BIRD.
YEAH, BUT JUST CAUSE THEY'RE A BUNCH OF MEAN PIGS...
VERY MEAN.
...WELL, WE CAN'T JUST STAND BY AND WAIT WHILE MEAN FOLKS DO MEAN STUFF...
EXACTLY, WE— WHAT?
...WHY, WE CAN'T WAIT AT ALL! WE GOTTA ACT! AND ACT FAST!
HANG ON, WE HAD A PLAN!

I DON'T EVEN KNOW HOW TO SPELL THE WORD!
OH, BOY.
I GUESS WE FIGHT.
NOW, THAT I CAN SPELL!
F-
-I-
-T-
—EEEEEEP!
BEAK
DON'T JUST STAND THERE, DECEPTIHOGS—DESTROY THEM!
WAIT, WE CAN WORK THIS—
—SQUEEK!
SKRUNK
BREEEP! FLEEP!
TUH-WEEP WEEP!
POOR BUMBLEBEE BIRD!
HE CAN'T TALK!
POOR US—THAT SQUEAKING'S GONNA GET OLD, FAST!

BUMBLEBEE BIRD!
SOUNDS LIKE MEGATRON PIG STOMPED HIS VOCAL PROCESSOR!
WELL, AT LEAST WE WON'T HAVE TO LISTEN TO HIM BEING REASONABLE ANYMORE.
YOU WON'T BE ABLE TO LISTEN TO ANYTHING WHEN I'M DONE WITH YOU!
WHAT?
YES, OF COURSE I'LL ALWAYS LISTEN TO YOU.
HE WAS TALKING TO THE AUTOBIRDS, NOT TO—
...
NICE MOVE, HEATWAVE BIRD.
CRUNCH
YOU WON'T STOP US!
WAIT, WHAT'RE YOU—
PIGGY ISLAND IS OUR HOME!
HOLD ON AND LET'S—
WE'LL DO ANYTHING FOR IT!
JUST GET OUTTA MY—
MY SECRET, MEGATRON—EARLIER, WHEN WE RAN AWAY FROM THE AUTOBIRDS—
WE SECURED AN ALTERNATIVE FORM OF VICTORY, SOUNDWAVE PIG.
—THE EGGS TOUCHED THE EGGSPARK.
WHAT'S THAT MEAN?
IT MEANS...

...THEY ARE CHANGED, LIKE US!
OPERATION: MOBILIZATION!
AWWW... THEY'RE ADORABLE. YOU FELLERS WANT ANY CANDY?
CRAGG
KRUK
CHAK
BWOOOSH
YOU COULDA JUST SAID "NO"...
WAIT— WAIT, MY LITTLE TASTE-TREATS!
YOU STILL LOOK DELICIOUS!
WHAT THE—?
THEY'RE MULTIPLYING!
PLOP
BLEEP
BLEEP

MORE IMPORTANTLY, THEY'RE GETTING AWAY!
STOP MY LUNCH FROM ESCAPING, YOU FOOLS!
WE'LL TRACK THEM DOWN AFTER WE'VE FINISHED YOU, MEGATRON PIG!
THEY'RE SAFER IN THE WILD THAN IN YOUR HANDS.
BUT... I'M HUNGRY...!
I'M HUNGRY, TOO—FOR JUSTICE.
NOW, MEGATRON PIG—ONE SHALL STAND, AND ONE SHALL FALL.
BLEEP BLEEP BLEEP
HOLD THAT THOUGHT—I'D BETTER TAKE THIS.
BLEEP BLEEP
HELLO? NOW IS REALLY NOT THE BEST TIME...
I THINK THERE'S SOMETHING YOU NEED TO KNOW, "BOSS."
STARSCREAM PIG? WHERE ARE YOU? I THOUGHT YOU LEFT!
I DID, BUT... WELL, THINGS GOT A LITTLE WEIRD.
I KNOW! MY TASTY LITTLE EGGS SPROUTED FEET AND MULTIPLIED.
ONE—THAT'S NOT THE WORST THING THEY DID...

...AND TWO— THE EGGS AREN'T THE ONLY THINGS MULTIPLYING!
PIGGY ISLAND IS UNDER SIEGE!
NEXT:
"REVENGE OF THE FOWLIN'!" OR "EGGING 'EM ON!"

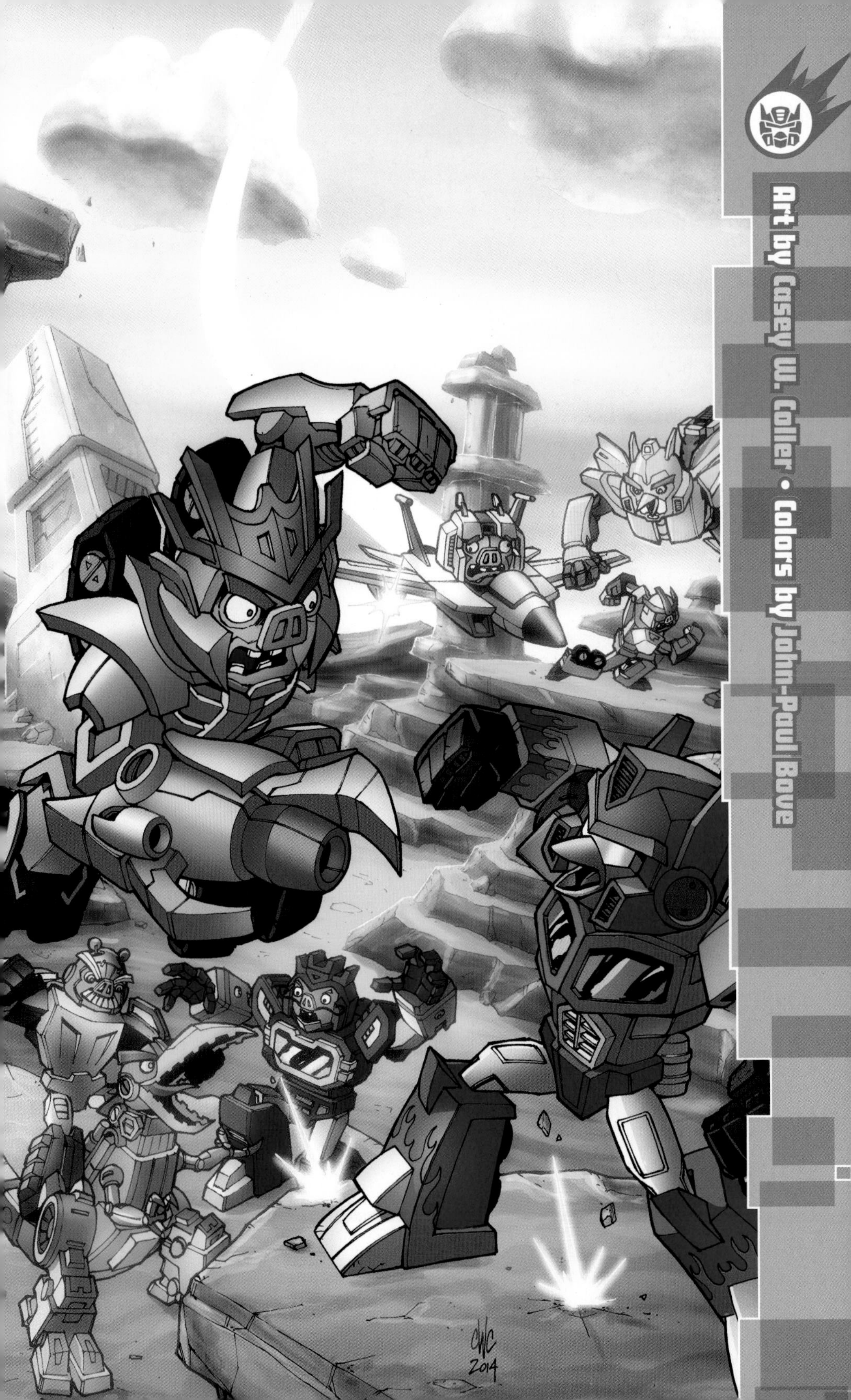
Art by Casey W. Coller • Colors by John-Paul Bove
CWC 2014

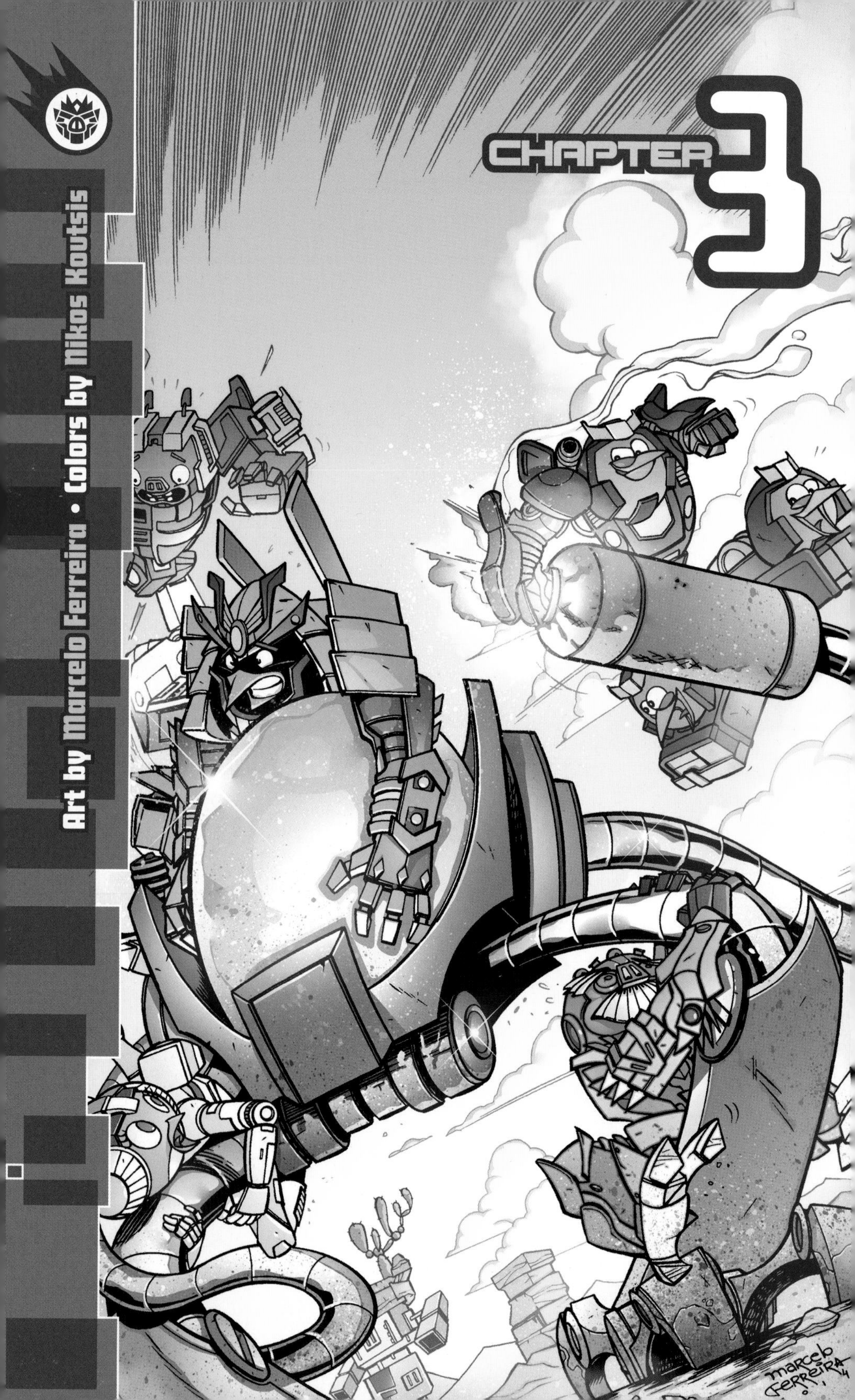
CHAPTER 3
Art by Marcelo Ferreira • Colors by Nikos Koutsis
marcelo FERREIRA

WELL.
THAT'S... NOT GOOD.
NO, MEGATRON PIG, IT CERTAINLY IS NOT.
WHAT?
DID THEY—
—JUST SUDDENLY—
—AGREE ON—
—SOMETHING? I'VE—
—NEVER SEEN—
—THAT BEFORE!
WHEE-HEEP!
ME GRIMLOCK BIRD DON'T KNOW WHAT BUMBLEBEE BIRD SAYING.
ME GRIMLOCK BIRD JUST WANT TO SMASH DECEPTIHOGS.
STOW IT—THIS JUST GOT REAL.
IF YOU PIGS HAD NOT STOLEN OUR EGGS, NONE OF THIS WOULD HAVE HAPPENED.
TYPICAL OPTIMUS PRIME BIRD. YOU'VE ONLY HAD FINGERS FOR LIKE TEN MINUTES, AND YOU'RE ALREADY POINTING THEM.
YOU'RE RIGHT, MEGATRON PIG.
AND YOU'RE— WAIT, WHAT?
AUTOBIRDS, DECEPTIHOGS— THE TIME FOR FIGHTING EACH OTHER HAS PASSED. NOW...

...WE MUST STAND AS ONE—
—OR ALL SHALL FALL!

REVENGE OF THE FOWLIN'!
OPERATION: DETERMINATION. THE BIGGER THEY ARE—
THE MORE DELICIOUS THE EGG!
SIGH... EXACTLY.
YOU MEAN EGGS-ACTLY!
HA HA HA HA

PWOOT
PWUUT
PWAAT
LOOK AT 'EM GO—
—WRECKIN' OUR BEAUTIFUL ISLAND.
BWAAHH! IT'S NOT RIGHT!
WE GOTTA STOP 'EM.
Y'KNOW, LI'L FELLAS—I AGREE.
THIS PLACE DESERVES BETTER'N IT'S GETTIN'—AN' IT'S TIME WE GAVE WHAT WE GOTTA!
UH. YEAH—WHAT JAZZ BIRD SAID.
IF WE ALLOW THE EGGS TO RAMPAGE, THEY'LL SURELY HURT THEMSELVES.
RIGHT, PLUS ALSO MAYBE SOMEBODY ELSE MIGHT GET HURT, TOO.
P-KWEWW
OPERATION: PROTECTION.
SURE, SURE—PROTECT THE ISLAND—
—SO WE CAN CONQUER IT—
—AND RESCUE THE EGGS—
—SO WE CAN EAT THEM—
—WHAT A GOOD PLAN!
A-HA! OPERATION: DECEPTION.
SHHHH!
MEGATRON PIG—THIS IS NO TIME FOR YOUR PETTY AMBITIONS. LIVES ARE IN DANGER!
YEAH, LIKE MINE—

—SOMEBODY HALP!
THIS THING'S TRYIN' TO EAT ME!
WELL, COULDN'T HAPPEN TO A NICER PIG!
THAT, STARSCREAM PIG, IS WHAT HAPPENS WHEN YOU QUESTION MY LEADERSHIP!
MEGATRON!
KWAK
OW!
WE LEAVE NO BIRD—OR PIG—BEHIND.
OKAY, OKAY, OKAY. SURE.
AND I THOUGHT YOU WERE THE REASONABLE ONE.
WE HAVE BATTLED FOR MILLIONS OF YEARS! I HAVE WATCHED YOU DESTROY CIVILIZATIONS IN THE NAME OF—
WHAT?!
I JUST WANT TO EAT SOME EGGS! IS THAT SO WRONG?
ME GRIMLOCK BIRD SAY "THIS GETTIN' GOOD!"
WHOO-WHOOP!
DON'T TRY TO CONFUSE THE ISSUE! THIS IS WAR, MEGATRON!
YOU WANT A WAR, OPTIMUS PRIME—WELL, Y'CAME TO THE RIGHT ISLAND!

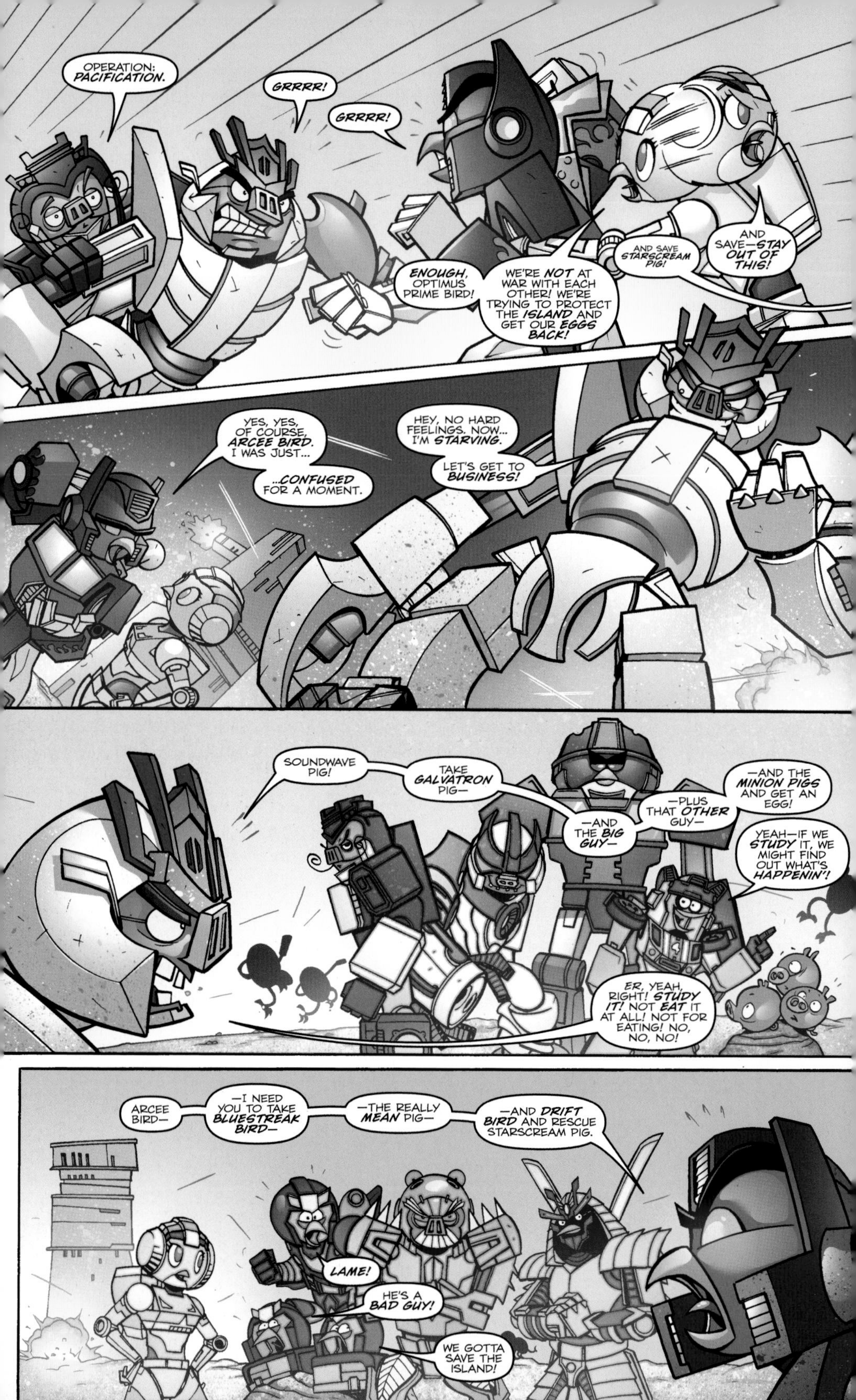
OPERATION: PACIFICATION.
GRRRR!
GRRRR!
AND SAVE STARSCREAM PIG!
AND SAVE—STAY OUT OF THIS!
ENOUGH, OPTIMUS PRIME BIRD!
WE'RE NOT AT WAR WITH EACH OTHER! WE'RE TRYING TO PROTECT THE ISLAND AND GET OUR EGGS BACK!
YES, YES, OF COURSE, ARCEE BIRD. I WAS JUST...
...CONFUSED FOR A MOMENT.
HEY, NO HARD FEELINGS. NOW... I'M STARVING.
LET'S GET TO BUSINESS!
SOUNDWAVE PIG!
TAKE GALVATRON PIG—
—AND THE BIG GUY—
—PLUS THAT OTHER GUY—
—AND THE MINION PIGS AND GET AN EGG!
YEAH—IF WE STUDY IT, WE MIGHT FIND OUT WHAT'S HAPPENIN'!
ER, YEAH, RIGHT! STUDY IT! NOT EAT IT AT ALL! NOT FOR EATING! NO, NO, NO!
ARCEE BIRD—
—I NEED YOU TO TAKE BLUESTREAK BIRD—
—THE REALLY MEAN PIG—
—AND DRIFT BIRD AND RESCUE STARSCREAM PIG.
LAME!
HE'S A BAD GUY!
WE GOTTA SAVE THE ISLAND!

I'VE HAD IT UP TO HERE WITH YOU, BLUESTREAK BIRD!
NO WAY, LOCKDOWN PIG! A CREATURE IN DANGER IS A CREATURE IN DANGER!
UP TO WHERE? ANYWAY, SELFISHNESS IS A VIRTUE!
HEY!
BUT HE'S—
—JUST A—
—STUPID PIG!
LET'S JUST—
—GET THIS—
—OVER WITH!
AW, WHO CARES. THEY GET BLASTED, THEY GET BLASTED.
THERE'S MORE BIRDS IN THE SEA!
...THE SEA?
I DON'T KNOW WHERE YOU PEOPLE LIVE. I'M A PIG, NOT AN ORNITHOLOGIST.
YOU ARE OUT OF YOUR MIND.
WELL—
WAIT!
DIDN'T THIS ALL START LIKE THIS? SOMEBODY RUNNING OFF...

—THEY'RE OUT OF LUCK!
YOINK
I REGRET EVERYTHING!
I DIDN'T MEAN TO MAKE FUN!
I'M SORRY I WAS SO ANGRY!
WE'VE GOT TO SAVE HIM!
WHATEVER!
THEM!
HONOR DEMANDS NOTHING LESS!
THEY SEEM LIKE BRIGHT LADS. I'M SURE THEY'LL BE FINE.
AAAAAGHHH!
DON'T FORGET MEEEEEEEE!
BURRRRP
WELL, THAT'S ONE PROBLEM SOLVED.

ELSEWHERE ON THE BATTLEFIELD...
HA HA!
GOOD ONE, VOICES IN MY HEAD—I WILL USE THAT LINE:
SCRAMBLE, EGGS! SCRAMBLE!
HA HA HA HA!
WHOA THERE, BIG GUY!
STOP, GALVATRON PIG!
BEFORE YOU HURT THE ISLAND!
OR US!
TRY TO LEAVE ONE EGG IN WORKING ORDER.
...
OH, BOY, HEATWAVE BIRD. I AIN'T SURE I DIG YOUR TONE OF VOICE, PAL.
THIS LOOKS LIKE A CHALLENGER.
WHY, YOU'RE RIGHT!
WHAT'S THAT? BEHIND ME?

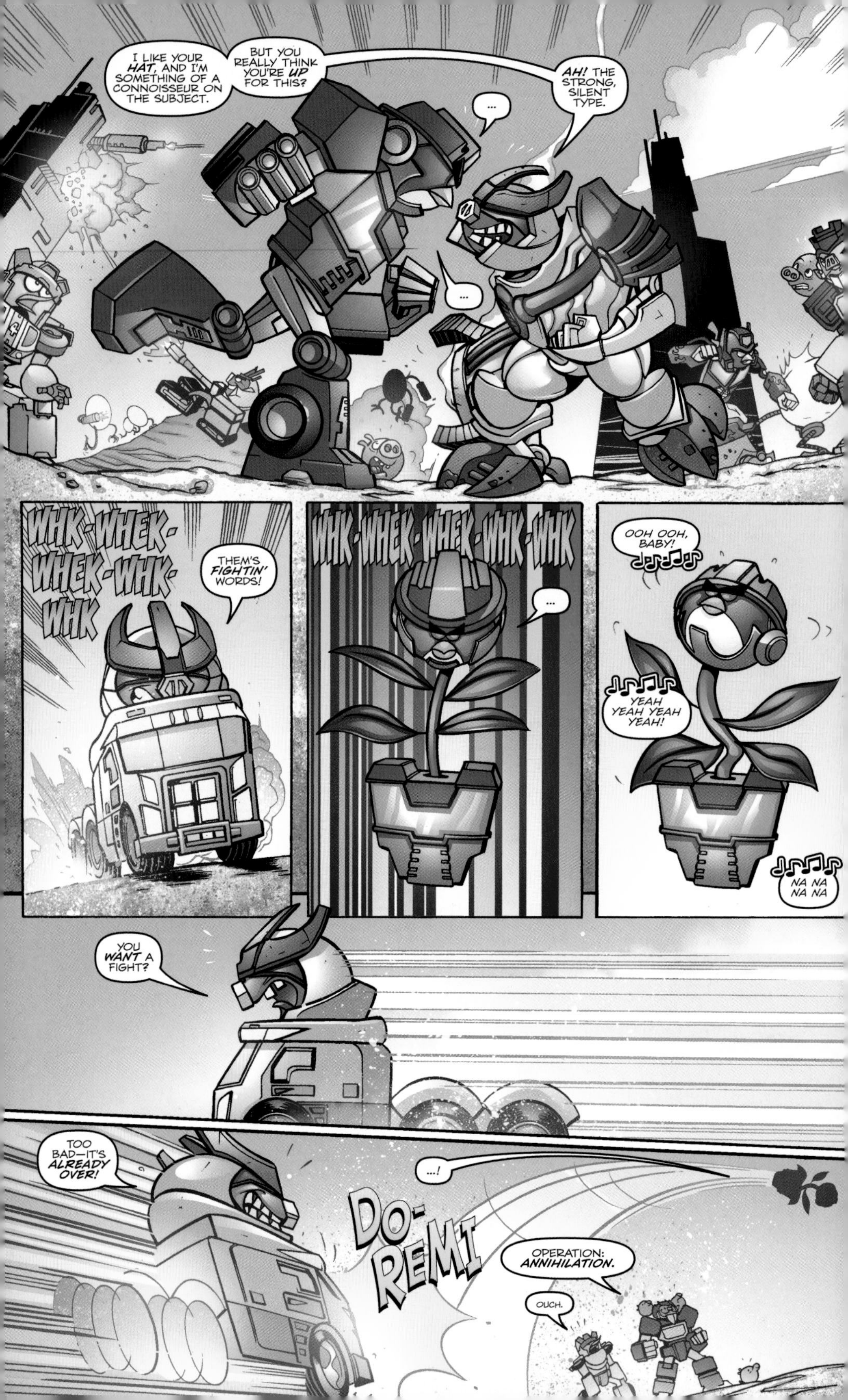
I LIKE YOUR HAT, AND I'M SOMETHING OF A CONNOISSEUR ON THE SUBJECT.
BUT YOU REALLY THINK YOU'RE UP FOR THIS?
...
AH! THE STRONG, SILENT TYPE.
...
WHK-WHEK-WHEK-WHK-WHK
THEM'S FIGHTIN' WORDS!
WHK-WHEK-WHEK-WHK-WHK
...
OOH OOH, BABY!
YEAH YEAH YEAH YEAH!
NA NA NA NA
YOU WANT A FIGHT?
TOO BAD—IT'S ALREADY OVER!
...!
DO-REMI
OPERATION: ANNIHILATION.
OUCH.

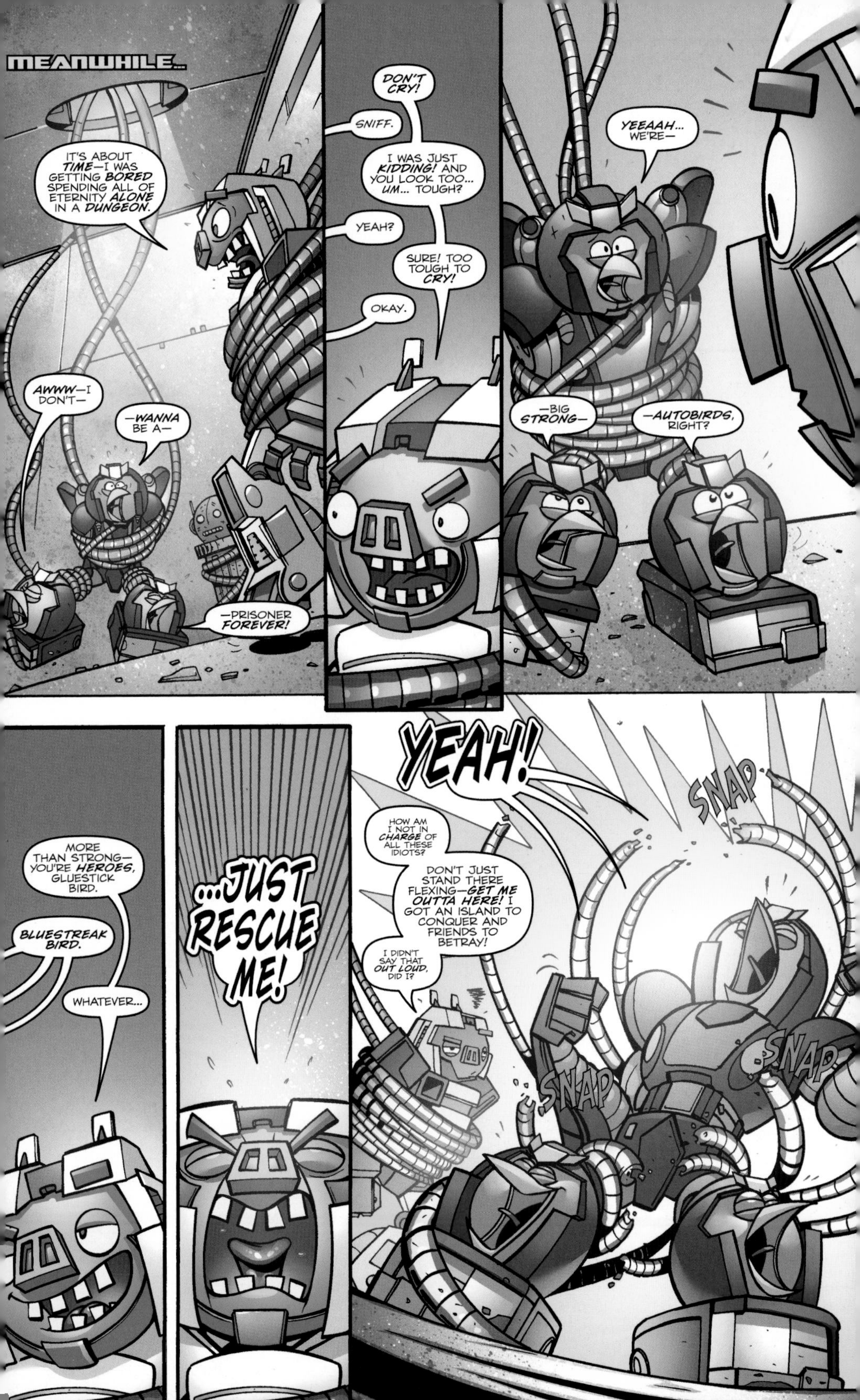
MEANWHILE...
IT'S ABOUT TIME—I WAS GETTING BORED SPENDING ALL OF ETERNITY ALONE IN A DUNGEON.
AWWW—I DON'T—
—WANNA BE A—
—PRISONER FOREVER!
DON'T CRY!
SNIFF.
I WAS JUST KIDDING! AND YOU LOOK TOO... UM... TOUGH?
YEAH?
SURE! TOO TOUGH TO CRY!
OKAY.
YEEAAH... WE'RE—
—BIG STRONG—
—AUTOBIRDS, RIGHT?
MORE THAN STRONG—YOU'RE HEROES, GLUESTICK BIRD.
BLUESTREAK BIRD.
WHATEVER...
...JUST RESCUE ME!
YEAH!
HOW AM I NOT IN CHARGE OF ALL THESE IDIOTS?
DON'T JUST STAND THERE FLEXING—GET ME OUTTA HERE! I GOT AN ISLAND TO CONQUER AND FRIENDS TO BETRAY!
I DIDN'T SAY THAT OUT LOUD, DID I?
SNAP
SNAP
SNAP

OUTSIDE...
HE'S PROBABLY THINKING OF WAYS TO BETRAY US, YOU KNOW.
HE LEFT US TO OUR FATES THE SECOND THINGS GOT DANGEROUS...
...ONLY CAME BACK WHEN IT GOT TOO ROUGH FOR HIM.
THAT DOESN'T MEAN WE CAN LEAVE BLUESTREAK BIRD!
WHO?
JUST GET OVER HERE!
WOMP
YES—HONOR DEMANDS YOU ADD YOUR FIREPOWER TO OUR OWN.
UH. I THINK MY FIREPOWER MIGHT BE NEEDED ELSEWHERE.
DON'T RUN AWAY, YOU DECEPTI-COWARD!
WELL, THE GOOD NEWS IS...
...YOU DON'T HAVE TO WORRY ABOUT ANY OF US RUNNING ANYWHERE.

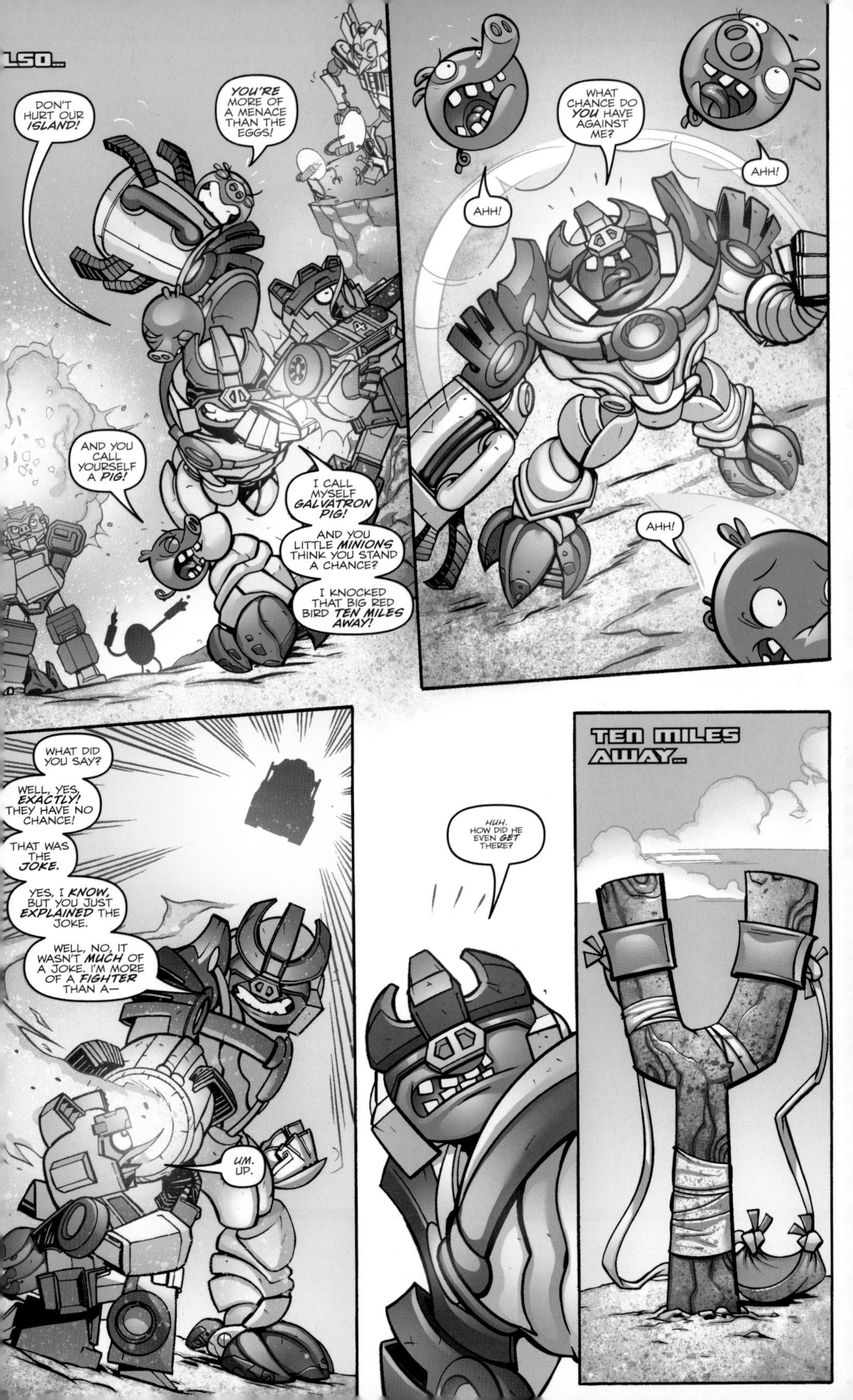

LSO...

DON'T HURT OUR *ISLAND!*

YOU'RE MORE OF A MENACE THAN THE EGGS!

AND YOU CALL YOURSELF A *PIG!*

I CALL MYSELF *GALVATRON PIG!*

AND YOU LITTLE *MINIONS* THINK YOU STAND A CHANCE?

I KNOCKED THAT BIG RED BIRD *TEN MILES AWAY!*

WHAT CHANCE DO *YOU* HAVE AGAINST ME?

AHH!

AHH!

AHH!

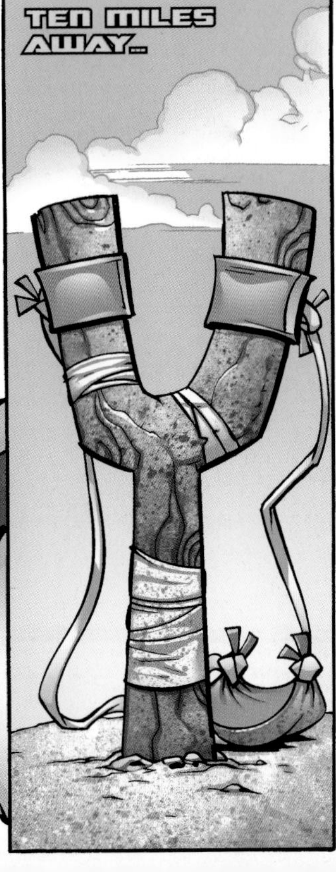

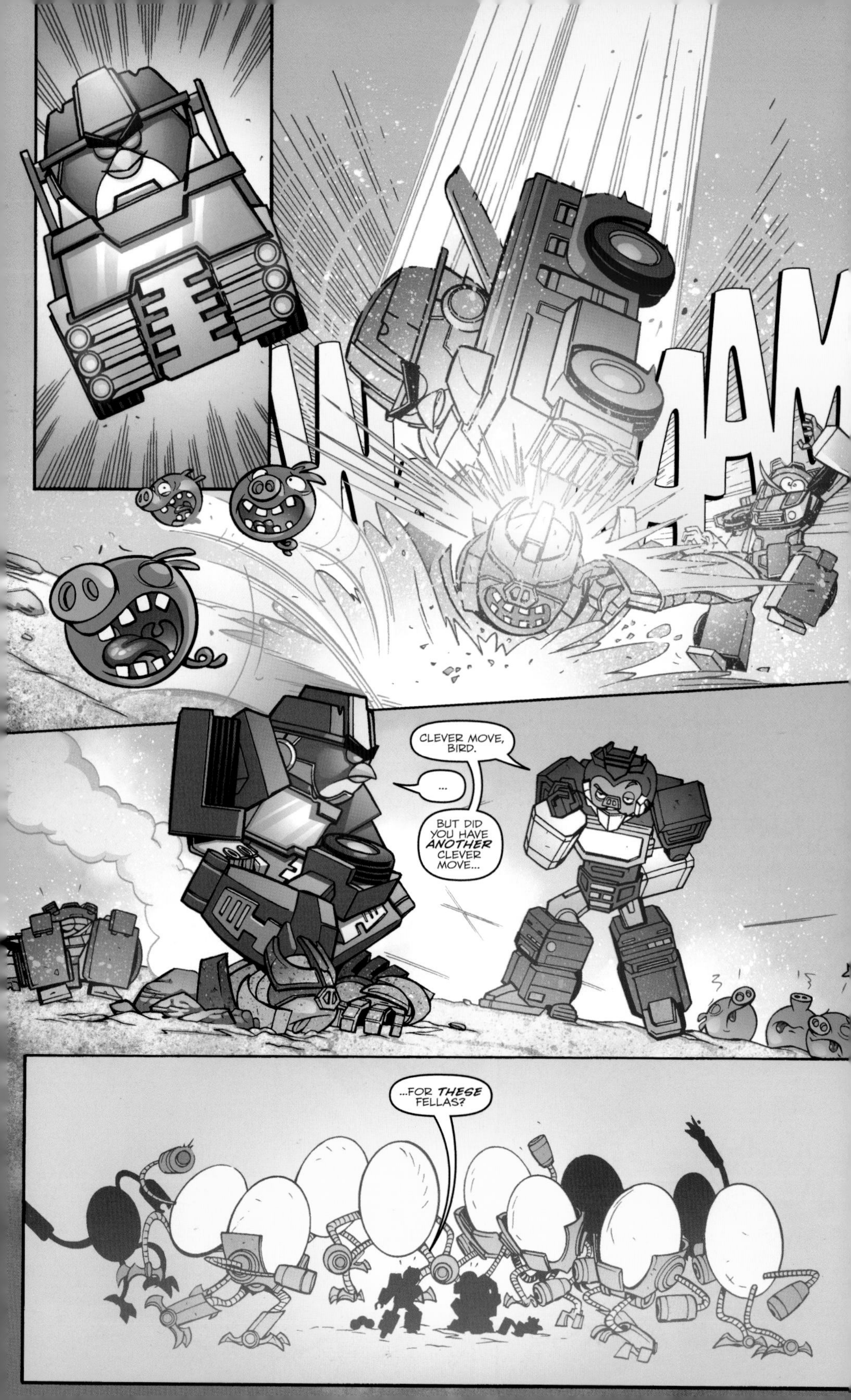

CLEVER MOVE, BIRD.
...
BUT DID YOU HAVE *ANOTHER* CLEVER MOVE...
...FOR *THESE* FELLAS?

PLUS...
WHAT A REVOLTING DEVELOPMENT.
YEAH, I HEARD—
THIS WAY!
—BLASTING OUTSIDE.
OUT OF THE FRYING PAN AND INTO THE FEATHERS, I GUESS YOU COULD—
QUIET, STARSCREAM PIG!
DO YOU HEAR—
—WHAT I HEAR?
I DON'T HEAR ANYTHING.
—GET TOO QUIET.
THAT'S THE PROBLEM!
A MINUTE AGO, THERE WAS—
—NONSTOP BLASTING.
—IT WHEN THINGS—
I DON'T LIKE—
WILL YOU STOP IT WITH THAT FINISHING-EACH-OTHER'S-SENTENCES GAG?
THERE IS NOTHING BUT NOTHING WORSE...

...THAN...
EEP.
...EEP.
...FINISHING...
RUUUUUN!
WAIT! WAIT FOR ME!
BOING BOING BOING
OW! OW! OW! OW! OW! OW! OW! OW! OW! OW! OW! OW!
WELL, AT LEAST I DON'T HAVE TO LISTEN TO THEM FINISHING EACH OTHER'S SENTENCES.
PLOP

YADDA YADDA YADDA...
EGGS! IF ANY PART OF YOU REMAINS A HEROIC AUTOBIRD—STAND DOWN!
OR AT LEAST JUST ZAP THE DECEPTIHOGS.
HEY—WE'RE ON THE SAME SIDE! WHAT HAPPENED TO HONOR?
YOU'RE A REAL EGGS BENEDICT ARNOLD!
BEEN SAVING THAT ONE?
JUST WAITING FOR THE RIGHT OPPORTUNITY.
I DON'T THINK THESE EGGS ARE GOING TO LISTEN TO REASON.
I THINK THIS IS IT, MY FRIENDS...
...AND YOU TOO, LOCKDOWN PIG.
PENG
PENG
PENG
WAIT... I HEAR SOMETHING...
SCRAAAAAPE
YEAH, IT'S CALLED IMPENDING DOOM, DRIFT BIRD, AND YOU'RE ABOUT TO BECOME AN EXPERT IN IT.
NO! THROUGH THE WALL, SOMEONE IS THERE—
GOOD THING ALL MY BLASTING WEAKENED THE WALL!
YOU DON'T HAVE TO TAKE CREDIT FOR EVERYTHING.

DRIFT BIRD!
ARCEE BIRD!
STUPID PIG!
YAAAHHH!!!
OH, GREAT—MORE EGGS! THAT'S NOT GONNA—
AAAAAAAAAAHHHHHHHHHHH!
—HELP.
I DIDN'T EVEN KNOW THEY COULD MAKE NOISES.
THEY SCARED EACH OTHER!
EGGS, EGGS. SO MANY EGGS.
I'M GLAD TO SEE I'M OKAY.

SO, THE BIRD IS FINE.
WHERE IS STARSCREAM PIG?
I THOUGHT YOU HAD HIM!
WHAT DO YOU MEAN?
WE ARE YOU!
—I'M NOT IN STASIS LOCK! I CAN WALK! I CAN EVEN DRIVE!
OPERATION: INSUBORDINATION!
AND WHERE ARE THE TASTY, TASTY—
—AND, UM, SCIENTIFICALLY FASCINATING AND STRATEGICALLY VALUABLE—
—EGGS?!
HAS ALL THIS BEEN FOR NOTHING?
LOOK— OVER THERE!
PUT ME DOWN, YOU OVERGROWN FIRE HYDRANT—

THIS EGG WILL PROVIDE INVALUABLE INFORMATION, OLD FRIEND.
...
I KNEW I COULD COUNT ON YOU, HEATWAVE BIRD. WE'LL LEARN HOW TO STOP WHAT'S HAPPENED TO PIGGY ISLAND.
THAT'S A GREAT IDEA. OR WE COULD MAKE AN OMELET.
LEARN OR EAT. WE REALLY SHOULDN'T RULE EITHER OF THESE WONDERFUL OPTIONS OUT WITHOUT TASTING THE EGGS FIRST.
I DON'T KNOW EXACTLY WHAT YOU'LL FIND, OPTIMUS PRIME BIRD...
...BUT I THINK IT'LL POINT YOU THATAWAY.
BECAUSE WHATEVER'S HAPPENING...
...THE EGGSPARK IS TAKING ROOT.
AND I'D BET MY SNOUT THAT WE'RE RUNNING OUT OF TIME!
NEXT:
"HARD BOILED"
or
"WHY DID THE CHICKEN CROSS THE END OF THE ROAD?"

Art by Sarah Stone

CHAPTER 4

I'M NO SCIENTIST—BUT THIS IS HOPELESS, OPTIMUS PRIME BIRD.
STOP BEING NEGATIVE! WE JUST HAVE TO THINK THIS THROUGH!
ARCEE BIRD IS RIGHT. NOTHING IS HOPELESS...
...NOT WHEN YOU HAVE HOPE, MEGATRON PIG.
WHAT? THAT MAKES ZERO SENSE.
HM. YES... MY INSPIRING SPEECHES SEEM TO BE... RUNNING DRY.
IT'S PIGGY ISLAND!
IT'S RUNNING OUT—
—OF EVERYTHING!
THE EGGSPARK IS—
—GETTING ITS POWER—
—FROM OUR ISLAND...
...AND OUR ISLAND CAN'T—
—TAKE IT ANYMORE—
—IT'S TURNING METAL!

THAT IS THE ANSWER!
YIPE!
YIKES!
YOUR INSPIRING SPEECHES ARE DRAINING AWAY.
OPERATION: CORRELATION —THE EGGSPARK IS TRANSMITTING POWER TO YOU, TO MAINTAIN YOUR NEW IDENTITY.
THE WEAKER THE EGGSPARK'S POWER SOURCE GROWS...
DON'T DO THAT!
I HAD AN IDEA!
WELL, CLEAR YOUR THROAT FIRST, OR SOMETHING.
WHAT'S YOUR IDEA, SOUNDWAVE PIG?
OPERATION: EXPLANATION—THE EGGSPARK DRAWS POWER FROM THE ISLAND, WHICH IS RUNNING OUT OF ENERGY.
THEY SAID THAT. WE'RE DOOMED.
LET HIM SPEAK, MEGATRON PIG. EVERYONE, BIRD OR PIG SHOULD...
...UM...
...TALK.
THE WEAKER OUR NEW FORMS BECOME.
INCLUDING THE NEW FORMS OF THE EGGS AND PIGGY ISLAND ITSELF.
OF COURSE! SO IF WE LET PIGGY ISLAND DIE, EVERYTHING WILL RETURN TO NORMAL.
THEN I CAN EAT THE EGGS!
BUT THE ISLAND WILL BE DEAD!
BWAAAAHH!
NOOOO! IT'S NOT FAIR!!!
WELL, IT'S NOT A PERFECT PLAN.

WAK
YOU'RE NOT EATING ANY EGGS, MEGATRON PIG— AND NOTHING IS DYING.
WE NEED TO SEPARATE THE EGGSPARK FROM ITS POWER SOURCE.
OW!
I WON'T MISS THAT WHEN EVERYTHING'S DEAD.
UNNNHHH...
...WHAT HAPPENED...
...WHAT'S THAT? DESTROY EVERYTHING?
THAT, VOICES IN MY HEAD, IS AN EXCELLENT IDEA.
STOMP
ME GRIMLOCK BIRD SAY "HOW WE GONNA SEPARATE WHATSIT FROM OTHER THING?"
UNG!
BREE-OOOP! PREET PREET FWOOT!
...
OH, YES, THAT IS VERY HELPFUL.
BUMBLEBEE BIRD AND HEATWAVE BIRD—I COULDN'T HAVE SAID IT BETTER MYSELF.
UGH! WHAT IS WRONG WITH YOU BIRDS?! WHY CAN YOU UNDERSTAND THAT?
THE REST OF YOU—THIS WON'T BE EASY.
THE FATE OF PIGGY ISLAND, THE EGGS, AND OUR VERY EXISTENCE DEPENDS ON WHAT WE DO NEXT.
ALL OF YOU WILL HAVE A ROLE TO PLAY. NOW...
...WHO'S WITH ME?

HARD BOILED
AUTOBIRDS— DECEPTIHOGS—
—TOGETHER, FOR CYBERTRON!
PIGGY ISLAND!
PIGGY ISLAND.
YOU SEEM UNUSUALLY QUIET, STARSCREAM PIG.
UH. ALL FOR ONE, AND ONE FOR PIGGY ISLAND?
RIIIIGHT.
WHAT CAN I SAY, LOCKDOWN PIG...

...ANYTHING CAN HAPPEN IN THE HEAT OF BATTLE.
SOUNDWAVE PIG—BE READY!
OPERATION: PROTECTION.
WE SHALL HOLD THEM OFF, OPTIMUS PRIME BIRD!
WAHH-HOO!
AND WE'LL MAKE OUR WAY TO THE EGGSPARK AND DISLODGE IT FROM PIGGY ISLAND!
HONOR DEMANDS NO LESS!
YOUR PLATITUDES WOULD BE MORE INTERESTING IF YOU HAD MORE THAN ONE, DRIFT BIRD.
I'M UP FOR ONE LAST JAM SESSION, OPTIMUS PRIME BIRD—BUT IF THOSE LITTLE BLUE FELLAS AND THEIR PIGGY FRIENDS DON'T GET BACK SOON...
I KNOW, JAZZ BIRD—BUT WE HAVE TO TRUST BLUESTREAK BIRD. HE—THEY—KNOW...

"...OUR LIVES DEPEND ON THEIR VICTORY!"
NO PRESSURE, GEARED-UP GUYS—
—WE'LL SAVE PIGGY ISLAND!
—JUST DO YOUR BEST AND—
YOU BIRDS DON'T—
—UNDERSTAND WHAT IT'S—
—LIKE TO BE A PIG.
OUR KING SAYS JUMP, WE SAY—
—WELL, WE SAY "WE DON'T HAVE LEGS."
THEN WE JUMP ANYWAYS!
BECAUSE THAT'S WHAT WE'RE BORN TO DO!
BUT WITH ALL THE CHANGES WE'VE SEEN...
...MAYBE IT'S TIME FOR US TO TRY SOMETHING NEW.
WHAT?! IF WE FAIL—
—YOUR PIGGY ISLAND—
—IS DOOMED!
SKREEEECK
CHANGE ALWAYS MEANS LOSING SOMETHING.
WE LOVE PIGGY ISLAND, BUT WE'VE NEVER BEEN ANYWHERE ELSE.
SO, SURE WE'LL BE SAD FOR A WHILE...
CA-KRASHH
...BUT—
—WE'LL GET—
—OVER IT.

SOMETHING THE MATTER, OPTIMUS PRIME BIRD?
IT'S NOTHING. JUST A...
...A BAD FEELING.
HA HA HA!
THIS IS WHAT LOCKDOWN PIG WAS MADE FOR—WHY WASTE TIME BUILDING WHEN SMASHING IS SO MUCH MORE SATISFYING!
ME GRIMLOCK BIRD SAY "ME COULDN'T AGREE MORE!"
AND, HEY, SORRY I BONKED YOU EARLIER.
ME GRIMLOCK BIRD SAY "NO PROBLEM, LOCKDOWN PIG"...
A BAD FEELING? REALLY?
REALLY?
COULD IT BE THE PSYCHOTIC EGGBOTS AND TERROR-TOWERS TRYING TO BLAST US?!
..."JUST WATCH YOU BACK WHEN THIS OVER."
ER.
OPERATION: DECIMATION!
I LIKE YOU. NO BANTER. JUST BLASTING.
...
NOBODY'S GOING TO BE BANTERING IF BLUESTREAK AND THOSE PIGS DON'T GET BACK HERE WITH OUR SECRET WEAPON—
KWAK

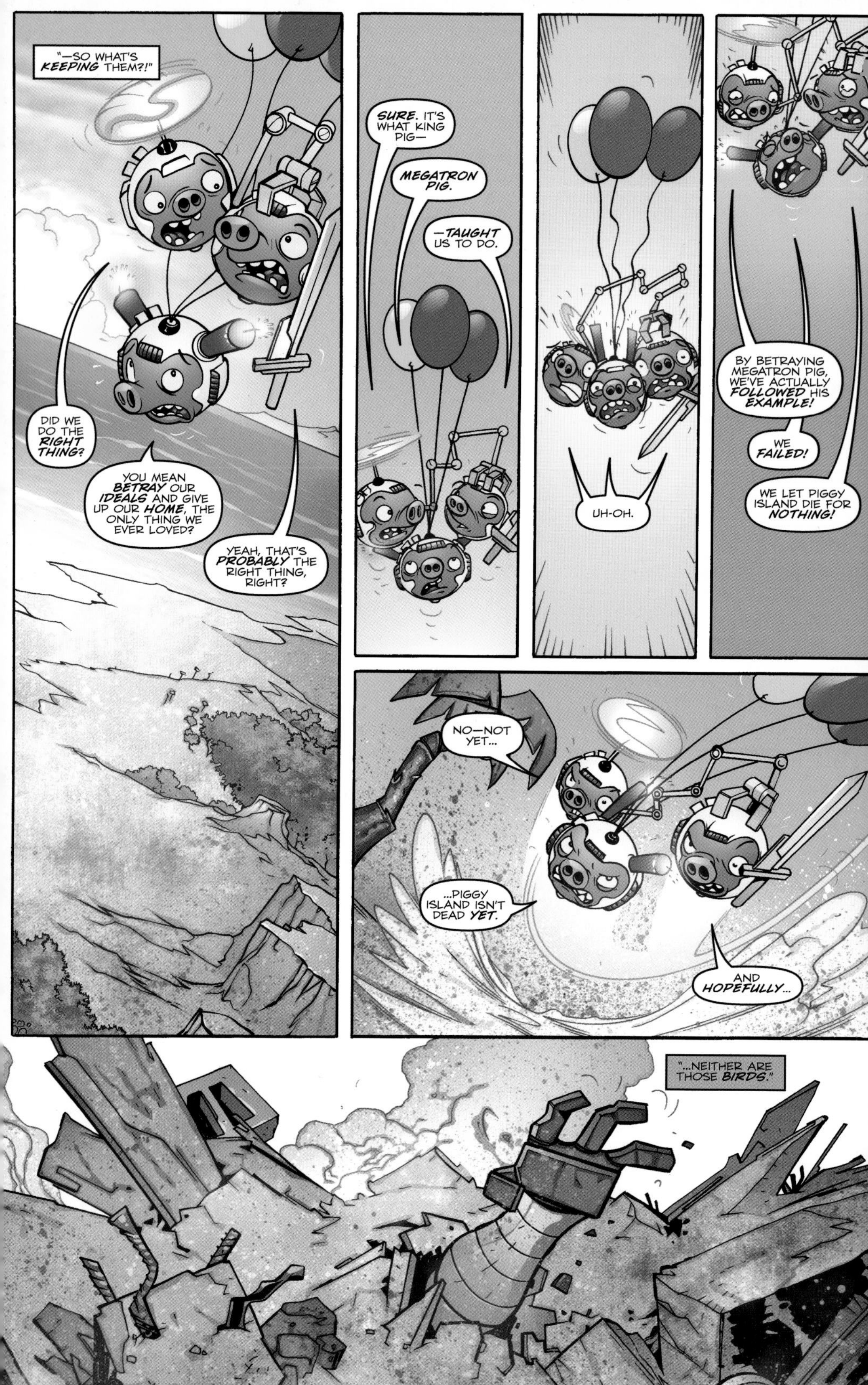
"—SO WHAT'S KEEPING THEM?!"
DID WE DO THE RIGHT THING?
YOU MEAN BETRAY OUR IDEALS AND GIVE UP OUR HOME, THE ONLY THING WE EVER LOVED?
YEAH, THAT'S PROBABLY THE RIGHT THING, RIGHT?
SURE. IT'S WHAT KING PIG—
MEGATRON PIG.
—TAUGHT US TO DO.
UH-OH.
BY BETRAYING MEGATRON PIG, WE'VE ACTUALLY FOLLOWED HIS EXAMPLE!
WE FAILED!
WE LET PIGGY ISLAND DIE FOR NOTHING!
NO—NOT YET...
...PIGGY ISLAND ISN'T DEAD YET.
AND HOPEFULLY...
"...NEITHER ARE THOSE BIRDS."

BLAFF
BLAFF
WAH-HA-HOO!
WOOP WOOP!
WHEEEE!
KEEP THE HEAT ON THEM, BUMBLEBEE BIRD! WE'RE ALMOST THERE!
MEGATRON PIG!
THROUGH THIS WALL IS THE KEY TO MY DELICIOUS EGG LUNCH.
I MEAN, THE SALVATION OF PIGGY ISLAND!
AND HOW DO YOU PROPOSE WE GET THROUGH?
SOMETIMES HONOR PROVIDES THE ANSWERS, STARSCREAM PIG...
...OTHER TIMES YOU MUST REMEMBER WHAT YOU TRULY ARE.
I AM A SAMURAI, HONORABLE AND TRUE. BUT ALSO AM I—
UNNNG.
WHK-WHEK-WHEK-WHK-WHK-
—A BOMB!
HOW'S THAT FOR A PLATITUDE?
HO-NORR

MIN-IONN
THIG THAD DID ID?
I GODD ANUDDER STIG...
UNNH...
...WHAT...
...HAPPENED...?
MISTAKES WERE MADE.
BWAAAH! SORRY WE BETRAYED YOU!
UH.
IT'S—
—OKAY.
HE WAS TALKING TO PIGGY ISLAND.
WE GOTTA STOP WASTING TIME—
—HEATWAVE BIRD TOLD US WHERE TO GO—
—NOW LET'S GET THE SECRET WEAPON—

"—BEFORE IT'S TOO LATE!"
I...
...I STILL FUNCTION.
WHAT'S THAT, VOICE IN MY HEAD?
YES. GOOD PLAN.
FA-WOOOSH
ME GRIMLOCK BIRD SAY "EH?"
GALVATRON PIG SMASH PUNY BIRDS!
ME GRIMLOCK BIRD SAY "WUH-OH."
WE HAVE A PROBLEM.
THOSE NINCOMPOOPS HAVEN'T RETURNED WITH YOUR SECRET WEAPON?
WORSE.
GALVATRON PIG.
UGH. IT'S ALL OVER.
WAIT—
—THE NINCOM— I MEAN BLUESTREAK BIRD AND THE PIGS ARE BACK—
—WITH HEATWAVE BIRD'S SLINGSHOT!*
*REMEMBER THAT FROM LAST ISSUE?

GALVATRON PIG STRONGEST THERE IS!
AHHH!
THIS HAS BEEN—
—A ROUGH DAY!
WELL. YOU CAN'T SAY HE'S NOT EFFECTIVE.
OW.
SPWASH
HEY!
STOP IT!
WE'RE ALL ON THE SAME SIDE!
DESTROY!
GET THE SLINGSHOT! GET THE SLINGSHOT!

DESTROY! DESTROY! DESTROY!
KER-WAK
ACK!
BWUMP
ACK!
ACK!
OW!
OOCH!
YIKES!
THAT SOUNDS LIKE MY CUE... HELLO, EGGSPARK...
...HELLO ULTIMATE POWER!
OW! HEY!
BWUMF
GALVATRON PIG WINS! ALL FALL DOWN!
NOT SO FAST, BIG GUY.
EH? WHO DARES—

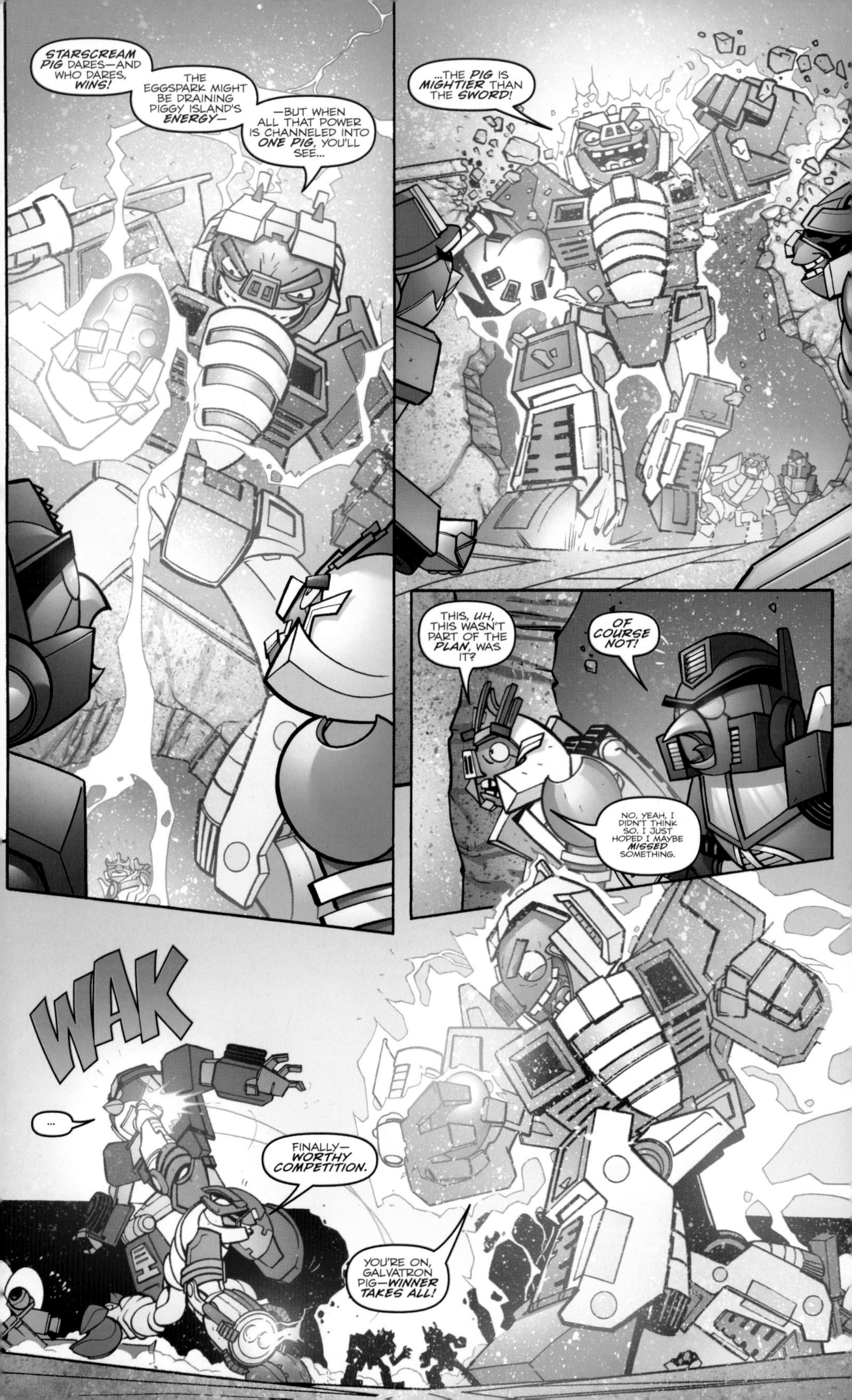
STARSCREAM PIG DARES—AND WHO DARES, WINS!
THE EGGSPARK MIGHT BE DRAINING PIGGY ISLAND'S ENERGY—
—BUT WHEN ALL THAT POWER IS CHANNELED INTO ONE PIG, YOU'LL SEE...
...THE PIG IS MIGHTIER THAN THE SWORD!
THIS, UH, THIS WASN'T PART OF THE PLAN, WAS IT?
OF COURSE NOT!
NO, YEAH, I DIDN'T THINK SO. I JUST HOPED I MAYBE MISSED SOMETHING.
WAK
...
FINALLY— WORTHY COMPETITION.
YOU'RE ON, GALVATRON PIG—WINNER TAKES ALL!

I GUESS IT'S ALL DOWN TO US. A SCHEMER AND RUFFIAN.
DO WE STAND WITH OUR ALLIES—OR WITH THE SURE WINNER?
ME GRIMLOCK BIRD SAY "WHEN GOING GETS TOUGH—"
YES! THE TOUGH GET GOING!
RAGGGH!
THAT NOT WHAT GRIMLOCK BIRD SAY, BUT THAT GOOD SAYING.
MORE APPLICABLE HERE, TOO.
NAB
STOMP
NOW! I CAN'T HOLD HIM FOR LONG!
SOMEBODY—DO SOMETHING!
IT'S TOO LATE, SOUNDWAVE PIG!
THE EGGSPARK AND ALL ITS POWER ARE MINE!
ALL YOU'VE DONE IS RESTRAIN THE ONLY PIG WHO COULD STOP ME!
WOO-HOOO!*
*TRANSLATION: "ACTUALLY, STARSCREAM PIG—THIS IS NOT A JOB FOR A PIG. IF YOU WANT TO KNOCK SOMETHING DOWN... YOUR BEST BET IS A BIRD. I WAS LIKE YOU ONCE: SELFISH AND RECKLESS. BUT I UNDERSTAND RESPONSIBILITY NOW—THIS IS NOT JUST ABOUT ME, IT'S ABOUT ALL OF US. SO GET READY, BECAUSE HERE COMES BUMBLEBEE BIRD TO SAVE THE DAY!"

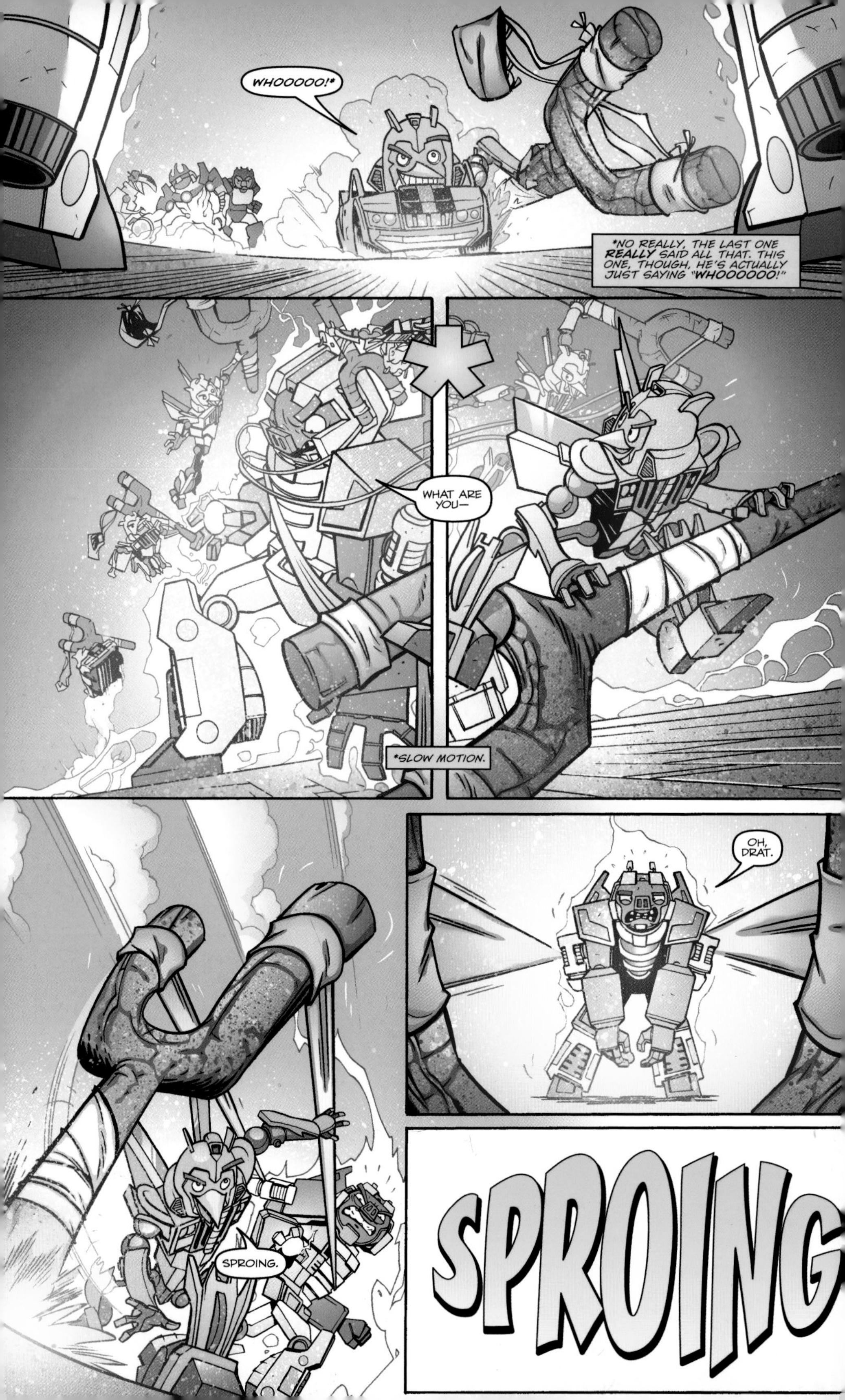
WHOOOOO!*
*NO REALLY, THE LAST ONE REALLY SAID ALL THAT. THIS ONE, THOUGH, HE'S ACTUALLY JUST SAYING "WHOOOOOO!"
*
WHAT ARE YOU—
*SLOW MOTION.
OH, DRAT.
SPROING.
SPROING

YEAAAAIIIGGHH!
GOOD WORK, OLD FRIEND.
I WAS GONNA STOP HIM.
WITHOUT YOU... FATE WOULD...
...SOMETHING SOMETHING...
...SENTIENT BEINGS....
FWEEP?
FIZZZZZZZZZZZZZZZZZZZZZZZZZZZZZZZZZZZZZZZZZZZZZZZZZZZZZZZZZZZZZZZZZZZZZZZLE
HUH. I GUESS IT'S ALL OVER.
ALL OVER BUT THE OMELETS, YOU MEAN?
WHEW. I LIKE BEEPING AND WHOOPING AS MUCH AS THE NEXT GUY, BUT I'LL NEVER GET TIRED OF MY OWN VOICE.
WHAT DO YOU THINK HAPPENED TO THAT PIG?
WHO CARES? MINIONS GROW ON TREES.
MEGATRO—I MEAN, KING PIG... I MEAN...
...AW, WHAT'S THE USE.
HOPEFULLY THE EGGSPARK HAS ENOUGH JUICE...

"...TO KEEP HIM SAFE UNTIL HE *LANDS* SOMEWHERE."
TIRELESSLY, MY *AUTOBOTS* AND I HAVE SCOURED THE *SPACEWAYS* FOR ANY SIGN OF THE *ALLSPARK*—
—THE LAST HOPE FOR THE SURVIVAL OF *CYBERTRON.*

STILL *NOTHING,* BOSS-BOT.
IT'S LIKE LOOKING FOR A *SPACE-NEEDLE* IN A *CYBER-HAYSTACK.*
WE CAN'T *GIVE UP.*
WE *WON'T.*
I AM *OPTIMUS PRIME*... AND THIS I *VOW*: I SHALL *SEARCH* FOREVER, IF THAT IS WHAT FATE—

—DECREES?
KER-SMASH
ME GRIMLOCK SAY "NOT WINDOW *AGAIN.*"

THE *ALLSPARK?!*
AND A... *GREEN PIG?*
UH. HI, THERE.
YOU THINK I COULD GET A *RIDE*...

"...I FEEL LIKE I'D BETTER STAY OUT OF MY BOSS' SNOUT FOR A FEW DAYS."
IT'S NOT MY FAULT... IT WAS—
I DON'T WANT TO HEAR IT!
FROM ANY OF YOU! I'M HUNGRY, I'M TIRED, I'M EGGLESS, AND THIS HAS BEEN A... A...
RIDICULOUS.
...RIDICULOUS DAY!
AT LEAST I DON'T HAVE TO WALK ANYMORE.
LEGS. YEUCHH!
YEAH, WE ALL DID—
—STUFF WE'D NEVER—
—DO ON OUR OWN...
...RIGHT...?
I DID WHAT?
GOSH... THAT DOESN'T SOUND LIKE ME AT ALL.
ME HAL SAY "ME DON'T ABIDE VIOLENCE, AMIGOS."
WE WERE ALL ACTING OUT OF CHARACTER.
...
MOSTLY.
I THINK WE CAN AGREE, I WAS THE COOLEST IN THOSE NEW FORMS.
AFTER ALL—I SAVED THE DAY.
WHAT!? YOU HAD—
—HELP! WE GOT—
—THE SLINGSHOT!
SURE, SURE LITTLE GUYS—BUT I USED IT. LIKE A BOSS!

WELL, CHUCK IS BACK TO NORMAL.
THE EGGS OKAY?
THAT'S A RELIEF.
SORT OF.
TOTALLY. WHATEVER THAT EGGSPARK DID WENT AWAY WHEN IT LAUNCHED.
I FEEL LIKE ME AGAIN.
ME, TOO.
KRRK
ZAP
AND I HAVE NEVER EVER LOOKED FORWARD TO A NICE, QUIET, NORMAL DAY MORE THAN I DO RIGHT NOW.
CHOOM
YOU SAID IT, RED.
I THINK FATE WOULD HAVE TO AGREE—WE EARNED SOME PEACE AND QUIET.
BWOOF
THE BEGINNING
OR: ACTUALLY, THIS IS THE END OF THE STORY. THANKS FOR READING!

Art by Guido Guidi

ANGRY BIRDS™ COMICS

WELCOME TO THE FLOCK

ANGRY BIRDS COMICS: WELCOME TO THE FLOCK

ISBN: 978-1-63140-090-2

Angry Birds, the world's most popular mobile game franchise, is now available in their first hardcover collection of comics!

ON SALE NOW!